THE
UNDISCOVERED
COUNTRY

THE UNDISCOVERED COUNTRY

SEEING MYSELF THROUGH SHAKESPEARE'S EYES

DIANE MEYER LOWMAN

atmosphere press

I dedicate this book to its catalysts. To William Shakespeare, who always knew just what to say and always said it so beautifully. To his words, words, words (*Hamlet* (II.ii.181)), which resonate with and inspire me. To the town of Stratford Upon Avon and its organisations and denizens who warmly welcomed this wayfarer into their fold.

"To be learning something is the greatest
of pleasures"

– Aristotle, Poetics

Contents

Prologue

"I like this place, /And willingly could waste my time in it."

As You Like It (II.iv.70)

I had a crush on a boy named Will. A teen thing—we saw each other on and off from middle school through college, but then universal forces flung us apart. We'd have sporadic, fleeting contact throughout my adult life. But I never forgot him, and those same universal forces also pulled me relentlessly toward him.

One day, at the speed of light at which time travels as we age, I found myself in a position to give Will my full attention. To try to rekindle what we once had; to try to infuse my mid-life void with meaning.

By age 55, so much of the material that imbues a suburban stay-at-home mom's life with meaning—or at least with busy-ness—had vapourised like the crew of the USS *Enterprise* under transporter beams: my marriage had dissolved, both parents had died, and my nurture-needing children had become independent young adults. I flailed in a vortex of grief, ennui, and anxiety, looking for a lifeline to pull me out.

While some seek refuge in speedy sports cars or extensive plastic surgery, I longed for a more intellectual challenge. I hoped to jumpstart my oft-idle brain to prevent it from turning to green Jell-O.

A friend's mention that her sixty-something cousin planned

3

to study Shakespeare on a graduate level at King's College London (KCL) the following year ignited an electric charge along my neural axons. I felt I'd been shocked back to life by the Bard himself, improbably holding a modern-day defibrillator.

"Will, Will," I thought. "It's you; it's always been you." Could my old crush extend his quill pen and lift me out of this abyss? Might he prove my ruff-collared salvation?

By some miracle and a lot of legwork in gathering age-old transcripts, requesting recommendations, and writing admissions essays, the Shakespeare Institute in Stratford Upon Avon (part of the University of Birmingham, England) accepted me into its MA in Shakespeare Studies programme.

Just shy of my 57th birthday, I sold a house, a car, and most of my stuff, and ran away from home. A newly minted expatriate, I embarked on my *senior* year: a broad abroad. I expected that this Elizabethan odyssey would stimulate my brain and my senses. What I could not know is how the year would force me—or afford me the opportunity—to examine myself and so much about my life, and ultimately to see myself in a new, refined, and more balanced way. The journey proved much more mentally and emotionally taxing than physically. I faced, fought with, and made friends with angels and demons that had danced around me throughout my life: the anxiety I inherited from my father and from generations before him; the symbiotic relationship I had with my mother, who was gone, and with my children, who were, in a different way, gone, too— to become adults; the grief over leaving a marriage, a home, a culture. So many brief candles, all burning out. I had to reckon and, ultimately, make peace with them.

The sound and the fury of the academic year and the consummation of the unrequited crush on Will obscured the nuanced effect of this change of venue. Only my sullen return to suburban Connecticut and subsequent return to Stratford allowed me to fully digest the pilgrimage's impact.

Maybe Shakespeare didn't make me change, but our relationship provided the catalyst that changed my relationship

4

with myself. He showed me what I could do and who I could be. I could not imagine how much I would learn about Will, but more importantly how much I would learn about myself through his eyes.

What follows is an odyssey through the events and emotions that had come to define me, and that I had to identify to make sense of and make peace with. This tale does not start at the beginning and end at the end. My year overseas dragged me from beginning to beginning, from end to end: the beginning of my family's immigrant journey to America, the end of my mother's life, the beginning of my marriage, the end of my dissertation on Will. What follows is more of a walk through a maze: it visits and revisits these topics, dips in and out of periods of my life, and drops me off, finally, at the end of the maze at the feet of the Bard who I so longed to impress—to embody.

Shakespeople

My fellow Shakespeare nerds,
wherever they may be.

Chapter 1:

Mum's the Word

(on Motherhood)

"A joyful mother of two goodly sons."

Cymbeline (I.i.50)

"I wish you would start your life." My mother lay propped on a mechanical hospital bed, receiving end-of-life palliative care. She had arrived back in Connecticut from Florida two weeks prior. The myelodysplasia she had managed successfully for the last five years had bared its sharp fangs, as we knew it eventually would, and morphed into terminal leukaemia. She caressed my hand and smiled softly, but her words stung.

"I *have* a life," I protested. Felled by a divorce seven years prior, I had picked myself up, dusted myself off, and cobbled together an existence in a universe parallel to that of the married Fairfield County couples that populated my previous world. I'd achieved my goal of completing Yoga Teacher Training. Before she got sick, my mother sat proudly at my new-agey graduation, her beatific smile implying more pride than the concern it did now. I had concentrated on my two boys' wellbeing in the wake of the divorce but had begun to focus more on myself as they matured and the trauma dulled. I'd been living a life, but never considered whether or not it was *my* life.

My mother drifted, then, thanks to increasing doses of morphine. She opened her eyes only once again—wildly wide—staring somewhere beyond my sister Suzanne and me at something we could not see with our mortal eyes. She clasped our hands with strength that belied her terminal condition and exclaimed, "My girls!" She died a few hours later.

What strikes me now, reflecting on that moment almost a decade later, is not the weighty sorrow of it, nor her momentary resurrection from a morphine haze, but the fact that of all things it was me and my sister—her girls—that made her eyes open and twinkle on the edge of eternity. I have no idea what other images danced through her vision in the rumoured pre-death flash of life, but it was motherhood—her progeny, her legacy—that both made her smile and gave voice to the last words she uttered.

My mother's deathbed words returned two years later, bouncing off the effete walls of the Virgin Atlantic lounge at JFK airport as I prepared to follow her directive. To begin my life anew. Sounding as vivid three years later as they had in her last earthly hours, her echoing message startled me as a spelunker's headlamp would a bat in a darkened cave. My mother had always been prescient, but it seemed that with her ten toes hanging on the precipice, she somehow sensed my future—*this* future—for me. I could not help but think of how it felt to stand on the edge of my own journey, to be without a mother (my father had passed in 2002), and to leave my children behind for more than a year.

Becoming motherless had served me a seven-layer cake of emotion. Relief tasted sweet: she had wanted neither to suffer through the fifteen-year-long marathon of pain and increasingly futile treatments that plagued my father as he dealt with non-Hodgkin's lymphoma, nor to burden us with her old-age care. She often joked seriously that when the time came, we should wrap her in a warm blanket and set her adrift on an ice floe. Which, in a way, we had. The doctors had presented her with myriad options for protocol trials for the leukaemia, but she eschewed them all. Ice floe time had come, and as devastated as we were, we had to honour her wishes. Also, we felt guilty, selfish relief that we would not have to watch her suffer either the travails of chemotherapy or the euphemistically titled tiers of assisted living. Moreover, my boys would remember the vibrant, silly, caring Grandma Barbara that helped them make Cheerio necklaces, served them ice cream for breakfast, and let them win at games of *Dots*, rather than a dotty, dribbling shell of that person.

The bitterer layer was her death's finality. My mother, imperfectly perfect to me, had my back 100% of the time, 24/7, like no one else ever had nor ever would. Losing my last parent left me orphaned. It laid me bare and unprotected. No more newspaper clippings on the subjects she knew interested me: yoga, nutrition, and, of course, Shakespeare. No more calls every day for a week prior to and on each birthday to sing in anticipation and celebration. No more absolute, inexhaustible interest in how my days went.

I often wanted to shout into the void she left to share something with her: the boys' achievements, a circling hawk, a bargain I'd found at Marshall's. I longed to phone her from that airport lounge to tell her that I had begun to fulfil her wish for me. I could only hope that my thoughts would somehow reach her like sonar would those startled bats in their dark cave.

My mom's mom was soft and round, with bosoms so big she refused to jog, claiming she'd give herself two black eyes if she did. She was also preternaturally cheerful and optimistic despite the struggles she endured as one of five daughters of Russian-Jewish immigrants and the wife of a Union City, New Jersey glazer. It surprised me, then, to learn that when my mother got her first period, Sally had slapped her hard in the face. As a longstanding tradition often mis-attributed to old-world Jewish mothers, it was meant, according to varying reports, to bring the lost blood back to the face, welcome the girl to womanhood, distract her from the menstrual cramps, and warn her off premarital sex. This one of very few insights into Sally's maternal style shocked me. I grew up reading *Our Bodies, Ourselves*, bras burning all around me, a sexual revolution in full swing. To me, Sally meant *kreplach* (Jewish dumplings) and musty lace doilies on dusty, darkly uphol-stered armchairs. A former seamstress, she had descended from a line of high-ranking Russian rabbis, but to me, she was simply Grandma Sally. As I write this, I sit staring at the samovar—an antique metal urn, gold and ornate—her own mother had carried as they emigrated to America, one of very few possessions to make the trip.

I imagine the shock my mother might have felt as she raised her own hand to the mark her mother's had left. I don't know what went on in her mind, or in her heart, but I must imagine she felt a sense of shame around menstruation; around wom-anhood itself. In the context of the overwhelming repression women faced in the 1930s and 1940s, when my mother was growing up, it would have been one more symbol that what her body did, how her body felt, was to be rejected.

My mother tended to simmer like Grandma Sally's famous Passover chicken matzo ball soup. Beaten as a child with a cat-o-nine tails, banished for "bad behaviour" to a dark basement that could have served as a set for every horror movie ever, my mother learned to keep her own needs lidded and her emotions hidden. Like that pressure-cooked stock pot, she would boil over, spewing invective disproportionate to our infractions. We might have only provided the last degree of heat to the roiling stew, but it was enough.

On balance, she was one of the best mothers I knew, despite her propensity to erupt when her demons surfaced and eclipsed her maternal compassion.

Visiting my father's hospice room, I placed a plant I'd brought to cheer him up on the television so that he could see it, as if it would make any difference at all to him in his deteriorating condition. It was clearly an attempt to ameliorate a desperate situation and my own distress. "Don't put it there!" my mother shrieked at me. She had dealt with his lymphoma for more than a decade, and most recently watched him nearly bleed out after a round of brain radiation that probably should never have happened. She had played caregiver to this stubborn, surly patient for so long that I doubt she recognised any semblance of her own life.

Nevertheless, her reaction startled me. "What difference does it make where it is?" I asked, her shrieky voice raising my adrenaline level. This was September 12, 2001. The television which my dad half-watched but couldn't really see played an endless loop of planes crashing into the Twin Towers, towers collapsing, and people running from atomic clouds of smoke and ash.

"I don't want him to see that stuff!" she screamed, her pitch rising.

"Well, turn it off then," I replied, thinking this a perfectly logical solution. But as her diatribes always did, this one defied logic. Neither that plant placement, the terrorist attacks, nor my father's terminal condition were my fault, but once she reached a boiling point, reason disappeared, and I received the blowback from whatever had triggered her.

A few years later, I brought my boys to visit her in Florida, where she'd moved permanently after Dad died. Her condo sat so close to the Atlantic shore that you could be looking out the window of a cruise ship. I don't even remember what provoked this particular tirade—Who would sleep where? Unpacked clothes left out? Decisions about activities? —but she stormed down the hallway of the two-bedroom apartment, screeching at that level that always made me both cower—a child again—and tune her out. All I heard was what the characters of the cartoon strip *Peanuts* hear their parents say: "wa wa wa wa wa wa." It tripped a switch in me, too. I'd had it. I'd *had* it. Enough of her yelling at me, and certainly enough of her modelling the behaviour in front of my boys. I knew I had inherited her predilection to explode, and while I worked hard at moderating it, I did not want to bequeath it to one more generation. I swore I would never bring them down to Florida to visit again, and I didn't.

My mother's absence and my own weighed on me acutely in England. In leaving the States behind for thirteen months, I'd given away not only most of my worldly possessions, but also the opportunity to see my children. While the flight might not have carried me as far off as death had my mother, the intervening ocean felt like the vacuum between galaxies.

Although by then my boys had grown and flown, we spoke and saw each other often. With the easy access technology afforded, I struggled, as many a mama bear does, with striking the right balance of post-nest parenting. The role of mother morphs as offspring reach young adulthood. They no longer want or require hands-on nurturing. They sometimes seek guidance or reunion. I worked hard to find the right recipe— neither too much spicy intervention nor too many treacly check-ins, no matter how strongly I felt I knew the best ways to solve all their problems.

I worried that both the Atlantic and the enormity of the work I was poised to undertake were tantamount to resigning from my mothering job. It'd be more difficult for my sons to reach me and for me to help them. I felt tremendous excitement and joy at fulfilling a dream and a wish my mom had made for me, but I felt equal trepidation and guilt at abdicating my own role as mother. I felt I was abandoning my children.

I knew they didn't see it that way. They channelled the enthusiasm I knew my mom would have felt. Perhaps I worried not so much about what they'd do without me nearby as what I'd do without them to worry about.

In a stroke of heavy-handed foreshadowing, my parents had moved, of all places, to the town of Stratford, Connecticut, to be near all their grandchildren (my sister lived minutes from me). What an omen—them living in Shakespeare's sister city, complete with a replica Globe Theatre (which mischievous teens would burn to the ground years later, much like a cannon blast did to the original during a performance of *Henry VIII* in 1613).

I felt my mother's presence everywhere in the original Stratford. Time had diminished any resentment I had toward her for her volatility, and I found her ethereal presence an immense comfort to me alone in this new place. For instance, the River Avon, which splits the town in two, teems with swans, particularly near the Royal Shakespeare Company where visitors—including my boys when they visited—fed them. Ben Jonson, a Shakespeare contemporary and popular playwright dubbed the Bard the "Swan of Avon." My mother and father had adored the swan family that paraded their brood each season by their small lake cabin in New Jersey. They dubbed them the "Swanskies."

Also, the Beach Boys' "Barbara Ann" played in frequent rotation in my favourite eatery, Boston Tea Party. My mother's name was Barbara, so I heard her name over and over because I went there so often to work.

Just over the six-hundred-year-old Clopton Bridge in Stratford Upon Avon (SUA) sat one of only sixteen butterfly farms in the UK. My mother loved butterflies—their iridescent colours, their fluttering, gossamer wings. She contentedly watched them alight on the fragrant lilacs she planted to attract and nurture them. After she died, one single vibrant monarch would often follow me up and down the crescent of sand at Compo Beach in Westport. A monarch had no business being there—strong beach breezes and an absence of butterfly food made their presence suspect—so I could only assume it was her accompanying me.

The hawks that graced the skies above her home in Connecticut, and later coastal Florida, also entranced her. She admired their unique combination of strength and grace and would point them out to my boys whenever they visited. She must have been watching over me in England, then, as the avian predators made frequent forays over the skies there, too.

Wherever I turned, whatever fauna caught my gaze, there hovered my mother's essence.

Before her nest emptied, my mother began to pursue some of her own interests, which no doubt provided a small release valve for her pent-up frustration. In her early forties, her baby brother had lured her out of her marital malaise to go into business with him at the Fifth Avenue location of a series of Sight 'n Style eyeglass shops he'd opened across the city. Later, she went back to community college. Her lack of higher education always made her feel dumb (she was not). She earned an associate's degree at age fifty in early childhood education, calling my sister and me frequently to lament and apologise for her poor parenting skills. "Pshaw," said we, wishing indeed that she had taken the classes earlier.

One of my favourite photographs of Mom shows her standing on the deck of their Dana Point, California townhouse, the Pacific Ocean a postcard behind her. She had just graduated and sported a cap and gown...plus a Groucho Marx glasses-and-faux-moustache getup. Her parenting motto from then on became "Be silly," and her alter egos—preschool teacher Ms. Barbara and Grandma Barbara—over-corrected whatever missteps she had made with us.

After my father died, she took to the road, flexing her new-found freedom muscles, exploring interests beyond those of his carefully orchestrated, self-serving itineraries. She joined Road Scholar tours to China, Russia, Argentina, and Croatia. Her terminal ailment aborted a much-anticipated trip to the Galapagos, which I hope to make one day in her memory.

I lost my mother once when she died. I lost her again after selling the home where we raised our two boys. Prior to the move to England, I accepted the need to downsize, and culled and consolidated twenty years' accumulation that sprawled over nearly 6,000 square feet to fit into a nondescript, easy-to-maintain apartment nearby. I stood surrounded by the material representation of what remained of the life she wanted me to restart. Nearly every inch of the 1,500 square feet in the new place was covered with my remaining possessions.

It was stuffed and stuffy and I struggled to open a window over a marble-topped side table that was covered with tchotchkes. I perched on tiptoes, tilting over the table to access the stuck window frame, and pushed with all my wilting strength. The window finally conceded, but so did my balance and I teetered as my heels landed back on the mediocre and slightly slick synthetic beige carpet. On the way down, my elbow managed to land precisely in between two identical Lladró statues that stood like two bowling pins, taunting me to score a spare. Bingo! I could not have calculated and planned the precision of my elbow's trajectory, but it took out both of these pastoral young ladies, both cradling lambs in their light blue-clad arms.

The twin statuettes that I had bought for me and mom on my first overseas trip to study in Madrid at age sixteen reeled backwards, landing just on the sharp edge of the marble top. I watched their heads separate from their necks and fall to the floor. I had decapitated not only my own souvenir, but the one I took from my mother's place after she died. Both of their heads rolled under a couch, into the shadows.

A child wakes to find her mother gone. Distraught, she begins a pilgrimage to find her or a suitable surrogate. P.D. Eastman developed this plotline in his seminal children's book *Are You My Mother?* in which a hatchling makes the titular inquiry of many animal species after her mother has rushed off to procure supplies, realising her egg's hatching is imminent. But this story, published before I turned one, might have been mine during my year in Stratford Upon Avon. Motherless, and in some ways childless, I subconsciously sought out others to nurture me and to nurture.

I met pink-haired Hannah in CV37 (Stratford's postcode and nickname) as I lay crying on a yoga mat. Classes at the Shakespeare Institute hadn't begun. I knew no one, and I was in the midst of a major struggle with a malodorous poltergeist living in my tiny loo. I'd connected with Hannah on the Facebook site for new students and when she'd asked about yoga in the area, I invited her to join me in the class I'd found.

Despite our age difference (she was precisely my youngest

son's age), we formed a preternaturally close bond that endures to this day. We shared a love of Shakespeare, a distaste for fools, and the same slightly naughty sense of humour. We suffered the slings and arrows of our outrageous master's programme requirements, as well as the thrill of the adventures afforded by living in a new place (she hailed from the north of England).

I regularly had to resist the urge to parent her. She had lost several stones since her high school days but would still bring chocolate orange bars or Turkish delight to class to sustain her through those marathon Plays & Poems A&B sessions. At the pub, she'd snack on Twiglets and crisps. My children might have had to suffer through torrents of nutritional advice as I earned a Ph.D. in Holistic Nutrition during their adolescence. She shouldn't have to.

She had her own mother, with whom she enjoyed a close relationship. I met her when I went home with Hannah to Hull for a weekend. Jan was a vibrant, slightly irreverent woman whom I loved immediately. She awed me in sharing that she'd joined thousands of others, naked and painted shades of blue, for Spencer Tunick's *Sea of Hull* photographs as part of the celebration of Hull's City of Culture 2017 honour.

During the visit, I told them that some of my maternal forebears had passed through Hull while emigrating. A font of information about her city's history, Jan took me to the spot where the immigrant trains arrived. My maternal great-grandparents, on their trek from Russia via temporary relocation camps in Poland, would have stepped out onto English soil on that very spot. In fact, on hearing the story as a child, I confusedly thought my grandfather had said he was *from* Hull. Transported from that depot, they'd boarded ships at the nearby port for their odyssey to America. I stood there with one of the many surrogate mothers and children I'd met along the way, in the place where, in some ways, my own mother began.

Until the day she died, my mother often sent me little missives to let me know that I was always on her mind—carefully clipped and folded newspaper or magazine articles in envelopes addressed to me in her distinctive script. I do the same with my boys: I send every word I come across about Bob Dylan to my oldest, or photos of redwing blackbird sightings to my youngest. Jan does this for me: "Saw *The Lehman Trilogy*," she might message me. "*You must go.*" She knows and cares about me enough to think of me and take the time to do something about it.

In between the Thursday lecture and the Thursday evening play reading, I went with a few of my Shakespeare classmates to the Mop Fair when it landed in SUA. Named for the fourteenth-century festival participants who carried mops as they enjoyed the festival to indicate that they were unemployed and available for work, it now resembles any local carnival: nausea-inducing rides, ring-toss, darts, and lots of deeply unhealthy, deeply pleasurable food. I held bags for and photographed my friends on the rides. I assured them that this was preferable to me throwing up all over them. While I watched them get tossed around on the oddly named Dance and Smile ride (they did the latter, not the former), a tween girl ran down the ramp from the ride, tears streaming down her face from beneath round, tortoiseshell glasses. She wore a Harry Potter T-shirt and backpack, and her hair could have been Hermione's.

"Are you okay?" I couldn't help being a mommy, even there, so many miles from my own grown children.

She wiped the tears from her cheeks. "I'm okay. I lost £10 over there." She pointed vaguely beyond me. "So I can't go on the ride."

Her distress crushed me. I wanted to take her in my arms and hug her and give her £10, but I didn't want to be *that* scary stranger her parents warned her to avoid.

"Oh, everyone loses money," I said. "And honestly, my friends went on this ride yesterday, and it looks pretty awful to me." She nodded her head, looking over at the long metal spider arms that were preparing to wave the riders about like cheerleaders' pom poms. "Do you need money? Can I give you some?"

She shook her head vigorously, and tears began again. "No, no, please," she said. "I'm okay, really. But thank you." I understood that this would humiliate her and decided that distraction—for at least as long as her friends were on the ride—would be a much better tactic.

"I'm from the States, but I'm going to school here in town," I told her.

"Do you live here? I do," she said.

"Yup. Right near Holy Trinity."

"Oh, I live over there," and she pointed in the direction of her lost £10 note.

"Cool. Hey, I went to Oxford this weekend, and you know, they shot a lot of the Harry Potter films there. The entrance to the library was the infirmary. Remember that scene?" I asked.

"Oh, I love Harry Potter! Do you, too?"

"Yes." I nodded. "You should go down there and see all the places from the movie."

"That would be great," she said, a smile spreading across her face.

We turned our attention to the ride, where my friends looked delighted, centrifugal force smushing them against each other. Her friends looked decidedly less happy.

"I'm so glad I didn't go on the ride," I said. "I'd have hated it!"

"Me too," she said, a bit conspiratorially.

We're in this together, I thought.

"Are you going to be okay with no money for the rest of the evening?"

"Yes, fine, thank you," she said.

I gave her a big hug.

"Thank you so much. You're really nice," she told me.

Now I wanted to cry. "You are too. In fact, I think your parents and your friends are really lucky to have you. I'm Diane. What's your name?"

"Amy."

"Well, it's really nice to meet you, Amy." She gave me another hug before she went off to explain the odd American woman to her friends. They laughed together, as only a group of tweens does. But before they walked out of sight, Amy turned, smiled, and waved.

I described the encounter to my friends, to a chorus of "Oh, how sweet!" and we went off in search of Yorkshire pudding wraps, which turned out to be delectable. As I ate mine and tried very hard not to let gravy drip down the front of my coat, I espied Amy amidst an even larger posse of giggling adolescents. I tapped her on the shoulder, and she grinned broadly at seeing me. We high-fived, and went our separate ways, together.

Ann sat next to me in the very quiet reading room at the Shakespeare Birthplace Trust (the organisation that maintains and schedules programming at all Shakespeare-related properties in town), deciphering inkblots that passed for handwriting. Her job was to transcribe these historical texts to prepare them for digitisation, enabling researchers to read them without having to travel to this remote corner of the West Midlands. The tomes over which she pored contained the story of the town and its environs dating back to Shakespeare's time and before.

Our volunteer shifts coincided, though our tasks differed. I did whatever the director needed me to—researching or setting up upcoming exhibitions, straightening treasure-filled shelves.

My presence in Stratford Upon Avon fascinated Ann, who, at least a decade my senior, reacted with an endearing combination of curiosity and awe. She often asked after my comfort: Was I eating well, getting out enough, making friends? With my own mother gone, it was rare that anyone showed such interest in how I was doing.

In December, the ubiquitous tins of festive Quality Street Chocolates sat on the reading room desk to herald the upcoming holidays. Ann asked when I'd be returning to the States to celebrate with my family.

"I won't," I explained. I had no plans to return until after I'd submitted my dissertation.

She digested this in stunned silence. I could see her struggling with competing desires to not pry and to take care of me.

I had convinced myself that solitude would suit me at the normally busy time. I would bravely forgo family time and festivities for the lofty scholar's life: PG Tips tea and toast with marmite, my quill pen set dutifully to the grindstone, my mind churning out ten thousand of the best words anyone had ever written about Shakespeare. So, I almost resented the email Ann sent a few days later inviting me to join her family for Christmas dinner. But marmite could no more compete with turkey, trimmings, and figgy pudding than being alone could compete with company.

Some of the butterflies from the nearby Stratford Butterfly Farm seemed to have taken up residence in my belly on Christmas as I prepared to walk over to Ann's place just beyond Holy Trinity. Their flat overlooked the picturesque Lucy's Mill on the Avon. I often walked just past it, never knowing they lived there. The boulders and trees surrounding the gentle falls sheltered myriad waterfowl and offered a pastoral vista to passersby. Ann's husband ushered me out onto the spacious terrace where we could hear the geese and swan chatter and water cascade. This, I thought, with the real-life spa soundtrack soothing me, was where I needed to be.

"Amazing," I said. "This is one of my favourite places in the whole town. How lucky you are to live here." He took the wine I brought—a meagre offering for my deep gratitude—and showed me inside.

I may have been 3,300 miles away, but the aromas wafting from Ann's kitchen transported me home. Turkey, potatoes, green beans, and other traditional holiday fixings smell the same on both sides of the Atlantic. Nothing can trigger such visceral emotions as certain scents, and for one disorienting moment I wondered what my children were doing. In their late twenties and single, both were in the early stages of mapping out their lives. They would both be celebrating with their father, his wife, and their seven-year-old in their home in Westport, as we had done together every year. I wished, just for a moment, that I were in Westport with them. Although they had both visited me before the holidays, I did not return to the States once during the programme, and I missed them acutely.

More and more wine disappeared, and our conversation meandered from healthcare to higher education to politics—our lamentable leaders, Johnson and Trump. Ann introduced me to traditional Christmas pudding, concocted from a smorgasbord of ingredients, skill, and patience. Outside the towering library bookshelves, outside the insulated caverns of my skull, outside my myopic focus on Bard analysis, I felt relaxed, looked after, happy.

In a word, I felt mothered.

I unwittingly mothered and was mothered during my tenure in CV37. Time and distance separated me more from my own mother and children than they ever had before. The camera, pulling up and back for a long, high shot of the perspective of both giver and receiver, clarified the nuances of maternity.

Back home, I often strove to facilitate my boys' journey across the bridge that spanned their childhoods, adolescences, and adulthoods, either as some superhuman Atlas carrying the whole bridge on her back, or a tuk-tuk driver shuttling them across and reminding them to keep all arms and legs inside the vehicle.

In England, I missed them, but I was busy. They messaged me either when they needed me or when they just wanted to check in. They magically managed their way through illnesses, job stressors, and relationship issues without my maternal intrusion...I mean assistance.

The impact of the separation on my stress levels surprised me in its inverse rather than direct correlation. My family often chides me for trying to carry too much at once. I schlep groceries in from the garage or luggage into holiday rentals in one fell swoop, imperilling the circulation in both arms and aggravating the susceptible muscles in my lower back. The Atlantic allowed me to let some of the burden go; to carry just a bag of groceries in each hand rather than four dangling from each elbow crook; to glide through town with just a wheelie in tow rather than with two oversized duffle bags strapped across my chest and back. In Stratford, I carried a lighter load, and despite a heaping helping of guilt (my Jewish imperative), I mostly relished the vanishing burden.

The new camera angle also allowed me to realise that, despite her flaws, when I "saw" my mother in Stratford Upon Avon, I always thought of her fondly. Wishing she could marvel at the butterflies with me. Wishing she could meet the Swanskies' English cousins. Knowing that she would be so proud of and happy for me. I have no doubt that her less-than-perfect parenting skills made me a less-than-perfect parent. But also, I know that she did 100% of the best she could with 100% of the love she had to give, as did I with my boys. Her faults were occlusions in a multifaceted gem.

Leaving my own children granted my mother's wish in

more ways than she'd imagined. I started my life, and so did they. My mother left me, but she never leaves me. I left my boys but never leave them. Mothering, sometimes, is not.

Shakesbeer

One of many products, in this case alcoholic,
named for the Bard with the expectation that his
appeal would by osmosis increase the appeal
of said product.

Chapter 2:

You're Making Me Anxious
(On dancing with my anxiety)

"Let us be worried."

Henry V (I.ii.220)

Any gaiety we felt heading out of the city came to an abrupt halt with the bus. We sat midway through the 1.5-mile Lincoln Tunnel, ninety-seven feet below the Hudson River's surface, partway through the 1981 winter. Several of the other recent college graduates in my management training program at Metropolitan Life and I had joined the company's ski club, and we were headed to Mount Ascutney, Vermont, for the weekend.

"This bus should *not* stop in the middle of this tunnel. You can't breathe down here," I told my friend Michael, as if he had any control over the situation. Diesel fumes mingled with murmurs of concern wafted back to us in defiance of both the bus's feeble air filtration system and the tunnel's behemoth exhaust turbines.

"This tunnel sucks. Traffic never moves," he said.

But by then, the driver had killed the engine and with it

any illusion that this was "just traffic." Each passing minute and gulp of automotive exhaust catalysed some chemical reaction in my body.

"Damn, Diane, you are lavender. Are you okay?" Michael low-key beckoned other group members over to check my pastel hue. I felt, then, as if I were watching myself: face ashen, heart fighting to get out of my ribcage, equilibrium thrown into disarray.

"No. NO. I need air." Somebody grabbed an elbow, someone else put an arm around my waist, and down the shabby aisle we went, soldiers carrying their wounded.

"She needs to get out." *I need to get out.* "She doesn't feel good." *I don't feel good.* I could hear them say what I thought I was saying but couldn't say because my head floated in blue cotton candy.

"No way, man, I can't open this door," the driver said. "Against company policy. Against the rules. I'd get in trouble, man." Overworked and underpaid, the driver was not about to capitulate to a busload of entitled, horny, uptight young professionals going AWOL for the weekend.

It's okay, I thought, *because I'm just going to die.*

My friends pleaded and negotiated while I wondered what it would be like to die in the Lincoln Tunnel. Would they take my body all the way to Vermont and put it on the abundant ice until we made the return journey? My poor parents: my dad worked at Metropolitan Life, too—would he feel guilty for recruiting me to his company and cementing my early demise? My heart strained against my chest to break free and smack the driver. "Let me out, please!" I thought I shouted, but my voice scarcely rose above a whisper.

The driver relented, finally, likely reckoning that he'd rather suffer a traffic violation than deal with a dead girl. He would open the doors, he said, if I promised to sit on the steps of the large coach and not put a foot onto the sooty pavement of the subterranean tube. I bobbed my head up and down in an assent that made me even queasier.

A week later, my mother and I sat in a New York cardiologist's office. In describing the incident to my parents, my mention of heart palpitations led them to seek out this specialist, who suspected a heart abnormality. But after reading the results of the 24-hour halter monitor (it resembled a clunky Sony Walkman) that I awkwardly concealed under my 1980s big-shouldered power suit at work, the doctor pronounced my heart 100% fit for duty.

"I believe you had a panic attack," he concluded.

This should have come as no surprise. My paternal Greek grandfather euphemistically referred to his own anxiety as "nervous stomach." My father didn't call it anything but attempted to numb it nightly with two fingers of Scotch. He also insisted everyone in his orbit do everything he wanted, when and how he wanted. In the days of a waxing recognition of mental illness, they called it Generalised Anxiety Disorder.

These bouts of anxiety ebb and flow like the tide, but without its predictability, as if the Moon's distance from the Earth fluctuated capriciously, causing greater or lesser swells, seemingly on a whim. Omnipresent, sometimes my anxiety laps like a lazy wave on a Gulf Coast cove; other times, it wipes me out like a Pacific tsunami.

The serotonin receptors in my brain, many professionals have told me, are like greedy little Pac-Men, gobbling up the feel-good chemical with abandon. The cerebral dysfunction results in an almost constant simmer of concern and discomfort, like the feeling when you know something is amiss the second before you remember precisely what it is. Selective Serotonin Reuptake Inhibitors act as a diet coach, keeping my hungry synapses sated but not overfed.

Today, I manage this with Cognitive Behaviour Therapy, Zoloft, yoga, meditation, and the occasional glass of rosé. But Zoloft debuted in 1992, and only entered the mainstream years after that. So, for more than a decade, I coped on my own with some therapy and self-help books.

Initially, my logical brain sought to manage it through confirmable cause and effect, imaging that would yield simple solutions. I avoided the places where panic washed over me. No buses. No Chinese restaurants (I had a particularly acute episode mid-moo goo gai pan). But skipping down that path led to agoraphobia, not a cure. I ultimately resented the seclusion and isolation into which anxiety lured me. I refused, no matter how uncomfortable, to wave the white flag and succumb.

Instead, I operated as if everything were perfectly "normal," whatever that sociologically assigned adjective that vilifies mental illness means. No one can see anxiety. If I'd sported casts on both arms, the world would understand how they limited me. Even if I had an intangible but more recognisable disease like diabetes, others could comprehend why low or high blood sugar made me behave erratically. Anxiety cripples invisibly.

"It's all in your head" couldn't be a truer, or less useful, statement. Well-meaning people who simply cannot understand how anxiety feels because they haven't experienced it dismiss and minimise the suffering it unleashes. Someone once suggested that the effort to explain a condition to someone who doesn't have it is like trying to tell a fish what it's like to breathe through its nose on land. Fish can no more understand the feeling than envision land in the first place.

"When I feel that way, I just buy myself a new lipstick," said a well-meaning but misinformed friend, trying to provide me solace. That word: *Just...Why don't you just?* Why don't you just fuck off, I wanted to say—as if I could wave a magic wand (or a credit card) and make this go away, but for some mysterious reason chose not to.

Six years of living in Los Angeles taught me not to hesitate at the first sign of an earthquake. Hesitating could cost precious time in seeking shelter. But when I felt a mental tremor, I did pause, all the time. Anxiety made me feel like a Weeble, those roly-poly toys for kids which "wobbled but didn't fall down." That phrase from the Weebles's ad campaign helped me assuage or cope with the scary symptoms: "You may feel like you're going to collapse, pass out, or die—and that it will last forever, but you won't, and it won't," my therapist told me often.

I had mixed feelings about being in therapy, but several factors had reanimated my anxiety, wraithlike. Sexual harassment had forced me out of a job I loved into one I'd generously categorise as "meh." My relationship neared that awkward tipping point of "do I stay or do I go?" I'd moved in with Donald but felt unsure about our future. And my parents, who had relocated to Dana Point, California while my father established a new Metropolitan Life office in Orange County, had returned with all their emotional support to the East Coast.

Back then, even in liberal Los Angeles, going to therapy was a source not of pride but of shame. No one talked about it or encouraged it openly. In practice, my therapist's words provided little mid-episode comfort—especially in Los Angeles, where, for me, a feeling of disorientation might be as likely to signal a surge of anxiety symptoms as an earthquake.

This discombobulation struck me one day, like a Zeus-thrown lightning bolt out of a clear blue, sunny, SoCal sky, as I sat on the notoriously traffic-choked 405 Freeway heading to Orange County for a client meeting. I didn't feel consciously stressed over anything, except my usual concern over punctuality and my general distaste for the cage that the barely moving cars created in LA traffic.

I drove a slim-hipped red Porsche 924S then, really more of a souped-up Volkswagen than the sexier, swankier 944. In auto-crazed LA, it felt like the sweetest ride to me. Previously, I had tooled around town in a claret-coloured Hyundai hatchback, often too embarrassed to leave it with valet attendants accustomed to parking Ferraris and Lamborghinis. The Porsche's stick shift gave me something to focus on in addition to KROQ playing the Fine Young Cannibals' "She Drives Me Crazy" (how prescient). I hadn't driven a manual since my father taught me to drive on his clutchless British racing-green Karmann Ghia.

Shifting focus can sometimes help side-track anxiety, like stemming blood flow to a tumour to stop it growing. That morning, I tried to concentrate on toggling the transmission in and out of first, rarely making it into second and barely touching third. But despite all my efforts to stay in objective reality, I started to feel that the shimmering blacktop waved like the surface of the sea.

I could often sense anxiety coming—like migraine sufferers get auras, or animals anticipate storms. I never knew how long it might last, how bad it might be, or how long the aftershocks would last. Thus, anticipatory anxiety—anxiety about the possible onset of anxiety—could trigger an episode as effectively as any "concrete" irritant. There, in one of the least convenient places for it to happen, I felt the dawning of an attack.

I sat on the freeway, unsure if I should keep going or if I should turn around and go home to curl up in a foetal position on the new tweed couch in our Westwood condo. I'd just moved in with Donald. I often ended days curled up there, wedged into the corner, trying to make myself compact and small, pinching myself so I knew I was still there, unsure if I wanted to be.

I drove toward the meeting on autopilot. In the meeting, every nerve in my body told me to run from the room and peel my skin off, but I stayed and struggled to keep that to myself.

I have always found it comforting to have sympathetic ears in which to whisper my anguish, better yet to receive a hug (not advice, not suggestions, not solutions) in response. When my father was alive, he listened from the east coast as I related my symptoms. Three hours ahead of me in actual time, he was light years ahead of me in managing this inherited blight. I knew he could understand it, but I knew it killed him to know he'd passed it along.

"I know, Klubie." Klubie was a now-defunct restaurant that sat on 23rd Street in Manhattan. We walked by it together on our commute from Peter Cooper Village to MetLife. He would tell me how he always found the name so amusing and had started using it as a nickname for me when I was an infant.

"We love you," he'd say, always the plural pronoun because he and my mother, both on the line, sat in separate rooms, holding different extensions (oh, landlines). She on the beige princess phone in their bedroom; he clutching the wall phone in the kitchen, no doubt twisting the coiled mustard-coloured cord around his fingers to alleviate his anxiety over my own. I could visualise his flat, ridged nails—as a child I'd mindlessly rub his thumbnail, self-comforting as if it were a worry stone.

"Breathe, honey," my mother said. An early adopter of the Silva Mind Control Method (an early mindfulness-based stress reduction program), she would wave new-age solutions at me before they became mainstream. She made and sent me index cards with multicoloured handwritten affirmations ("You're going to be okay!") on one side and encouraging philosophical messages that she'd clipped from magazines cut out and taped to the reverse. I still carry them in my wallet to this day.

Other people were less compassionate. It wasn't that they didn't care, they just didn't have the tools to support me. I didn't dare tell my boss. Looking back, I may have done him and myself a disservice by keeping quiet. Maybe it would have helped both of us to explain why I sat through that meeting, and countless others like it, distracted as I fought to stay and concentrate and make some pitch or presentation about inter-national employee benefits to Mattel or Security Pacific Bank or some other client or client-to-be. The buttoned-up, serious executive could have modelled for Brooks Brothers or the Republican Party. He was the epitome of *all business*. I assumed he wouldn't have understood.

My boyfriend/fiancé/husband/ex-husband tried his best to empathise and help, but often fell short. He was raised in a Southern Baptist family where no one ever got too happy or too sad. Stoicism and a stiff upper lip assisted by a *de rigeur* 5 p.m. cocktail hour kept emotions at bay. His exquisitely analytic mind solved any linear problem efficiently; my amorphous Ariel of an ailment fell outside his expertise. This didn't make him a bad person. This just made him unable to fully understand my anguish, and that frustrated me because I lived a continent away from my other friends and family and looked to him to be my Rock of Gibraltar. He was a rock, but just could not be mine.

"What do you think is causing it this time?" he'd ask, trying to help in the only way he could. As I had in the early days, he thought in terms of cause and effect. *If I knew, I'd make it stop*, I thought. Rather than a hug, he would tiptoe around me as I lay balled up on that sofa, no doubt silently repeating the well-worn adages of "This too shall pass," or more Britishly, "Keep calm and carry on."

During the months and days leading up to the finalisation of my divorce, all the SSRIs in the world were no match for the disquietude. My now ex-husband and I sat together (during the most amicable divorce in history) outside the Bridgeport, Connecticut courtroom on a worn wooden bench flanked by attorneys who syphoned money from us as thirstily as my synapses sucked back serotonin. We stared at the worn grey linoleum floor. My brain had turned to cooked cream of wheat. I could not feel the clothes on my body or the shoes on my feet.

I thought I stood. I thought I told them I needed the restroom from somewhere far away through grey cotton candy. I only knew with certainty that I had begun to walk because I could hear the heels I'd worn—to impress the judge? To look my best for the big day?—clicking on the floor. Now they felt like unsecured stilts. I have to assume my body switched to auto-pilot and relied on muscle memory because I had and have no recollection of completing the motor functions involved with removing and replacing the necessary clothing, urinating, flushing the toilet, and washing my hands. I could only assume they happened—as I assume I sat on the witness stand and spoke cohesively to the judge, hugged my newly minted ex-husband goodbye in the parking lot, and fell into my mother's empathetic arms when I got home. I had completely dissociated, and for that whole day had to resist the urge to ask people, "Am I here? Are you?"

A Partial List of Possible Anxiety Symptoms

Light-headedness	Sleep distruption
Difficulty focusing	Irritability
Shakiness	Hair loss
Globus (sensation of a lump in the throat)	Lack of energy
Fidgetiness	Fear
Worry	Sweating
Restlessness	Racing heart
Appetite changes	Headache
Lack of interest in sex	Emotional swings
Avoidance of social situations	Shaky voice
Blushing/flushing	Muscle aches/pains
Fuzzy memory	Impatience
Green stool due to excessive bile	Dry mouth
Need to urinate frequently	Diarrhoea

In the years after I split from him (and myself), I sat with and became myself again. I had watched many divorced friends sink into cesspools of hatred for their exes while plotting revenge through plastic surgery, or dive headlong into tidepools of rebound relationships that ended up as bad as or worse than the marriages they'd left. Some did both. I discovered that being by and true to myself was almost as effective at quelling my mental illness as Zoloft.

I weathered the sale and attendant downsizing of the house where we raised our boys surprisingly well. Shedding stuff associated with a failed marriage and years of sublimation of my own needs proved more liberating than anguishing. I gave away or sold everything that would not fit into my new compact apartment and felt lighter for it. I sorted through memorabilia from both boys' K-12 years—small handprints stamped in red fingerpaint transformed into turkeys for Thanksgiving; Little League trophies—stowed it all in lidded Rubbermaid bins and delivered them to their dad's place. I kept what I needed, learning in the process (as I did when I unintentionally decapitated twin Lladró statues) that *things* are not the people, memories, or emotions associated with them. "It's just stuff," as my mother would say, and the stuff I kept represented *me*.

I had to prune yet again to minimise what went into storage in preparation for my senior year abroad. This time, no matter how much I'd learned about the irrelevance of material possessions, the process re-stoked the anxiety flames. It wasn't so much letting go of the items as what it represented: this fantasy, which I'd concocted and executed impetuously, had become as concrete as the shoes with which Mafiosos allegedly dispatch enemies to the murky waters of the East River.

By the time the movers packed the final box and cloaked the last piece of furniture in cling wrap to keep it dust-free in storage, I moved to, of all places, my ex's home. He and his wife, with whom I had, by then, a warm relationship, had agreed to let me store some items and stay in their guest suite for the three days prior to my flight.

With nothing but idle waiting time (the ajar door into which anxiety loves to slip its nefarious toe), I said goodbye to everyone who cared that I was leaving, spent hours on the phone with utility companies, and checked and rechecked every detail of every stage of the trip on both the US and UK sides. All that was left to do was wonder what the *fuck* I was actually thinking and why I had the audacity to believe that upending my life, leaving my family and friends, and enrolling in a graduate program at the preeminent institution for Shakespeare Studies in the world in a foreign country was an even remotely sane idea.

The doubt and fear grew from the proverbial princess's mattress pea to a full-blown wild neurological ganglia dance. That familiar, unpleasant, and uncontrollable feeling of sliding out of my body and into a bubble of plasmatic disconnection returned.

I recall standing on the stairs of my ex's white house on a sunny, warm day in August as the driver approached (mercifully carly) and hugging my youngest son goodbye. I recall choking up, overwhelmed by the enormity of the moment.

Directions
< OPEN
PUSH DOWN & TURN
> CLOSE
Rx #: xxxxxxx
LOWMAN, DIANE
TAKE ONE TABLET BY MOUTH DAILY
Sertraline HCL 100MG tablet
Generic for Zoloft 100MG tablet
Qty: 90Refills: 0
Dr. Sarfraz, Naeem

Several weeks prior to departure, I sat in Doctor Sarfraz's office, feet dangling and swinging since they didn't reach the step up to the examining table on which I sat. I'd come to ask him for a year's worth of Zoloft and what to do if I got bronchitis in England.

Leaving him, my general practitioner of twenty-five years, caused my anxiety to spike like the mercury in the old-fashioned thermometer that my mom would place under my tongue—or somewhere much less comfortable. He knew me so well. Knew that when I got poison ivy—or even caught a whiff of it—it would spread like a wildfire in the California Inland Empire fanned by the Santa Ana winds. He would prescribe prednisone to quell the inflammation. He knew that if I even thought about getting a cold—before I could even feel the tickle in my throat—my lungs would precipitously shut down for business due to bronchitis. He called it "hidden asthma" and said it was akin to an allergic reaction to a cold virus. He would prescribe prednisone to quell the inflammation. He knew about my anxiety, and that illness triggered it. He had prescribed the Zoloft, held my hand, and navigated the minefield in my mind by helping me distinguish between anxiety-related and less idiopathic symptoms.

"What will I do without you?" I whined.

"You know, Diane, there are doctors in England," he reassured me without a hint of sarcasm. "In fact, my brother practices there."

I brightened up like a drug addict finding a new dealer after hers has gone to prison.

"He's a breast surgeon. You call him 'Mr. Sarfraz,' though, not 'doctor.' They call surgeons 'Mr.' there."

I deflated as the fantasy of my new supplier evaporated before he'd even materialised.

"Here's what we'll do." His calm always helped assuage

my lack thereof. "I'll prescribe one round of prednisone and a Z-pack so that the first time you get sick you will have it with you. And I can get you a six-month supply of 100mg Zoloft with a travel waiver from the insurance company. Since you currently only use 50mg a day, that should last you for the year."

We both knew that the UK had SSRIs, but also that people react differently to different ones, and neither of us wanted to risk upsetting the serotonin apple cart.

"And Diane. If you get bronchitis more than once, find a doctor. And have a wonderful time."

Find a doctor. Find a doctor. Find a doctor was all I heard.

I took the Zoloft religiously after I arrived and coped with the vagaries of the transition: getting to the root of and eliminating the odour of decaying bodies and feline urine that emanated from the tiny loo in my flat, learning the language, remembering how to "student."

After about the first month, though, I stopped. Just like that. Just like they tell you not to. Not abruptly, but I'd forget to take a pill every few days, and then more often because, well, I forgot I needed them.

<u>Shakespeareland</u>

Stratford Upon Avon and its environs.

Chapter 3:

Bardolatry
(On Shakesworship)

"Was this the idol that you worship so?"

Two Gentlemen of Verona (II.iv.131)

I sat on the stone step of the chancel, close to Shakespeare. Hushed light suffused the room, filtering in through the stained-glass windows. Tourists milled about, whispering in church-soft voices. Some did not even notice me—my back to the wall, slightly bent in reverence, my palm splayed face down on the cool slate at his feet. Maybe they read the book on a nearby stand containing the church's records, held open to the page noting his birth by a protective slice of Lucite. Or maybe they scanned the inscription in the stone that he penned himself:

> *Good frend for Jesus sake forbeare,*
> *To digg the dust encloased here.*
> *Blessed be the man that spares thes stones*
> *And cursed be he that moves my bones.*

He held vigil over himself from above. Dutch Sculptor Gerard Johnson's bizarre bust of him holding a real quill pen in one hand and a sheaf of paper under the other might have watched—and cursed—the opportunists who purportedly stole his skull in 1794 in the ultimate mercenary reaction to rampant Bardolotry. An exhaustive search for said cranium and 21st-century technology all but confirmed that the alleged grave robbery is as much a myth as many others that swirl around idols to, and beyond, their graves.

By September 2018, I had handed in my dissertation and the keys to the flat, and I'd come to say goodbye. I raised my head and lifted my hand from the stone. My body heat had penetrated the cold, hard surface and left an impression like the handprint a pre-schooler might press into yellow finger-paint and then onto construction paper. I took it as an ephemeral reciprocation of the impression he'd left on me. I watched until it evaporated, tears rolling down my cheeks, fully aware that by now the other visitors were likely warning their children to stay away from the crazy crying lady in the corner.

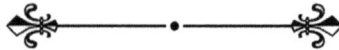

I don't remember a time when I didn't love Shakespeare. Surely, I would not have made more than a casual acquaintance with him before Ms. Robb's eighth-grade English class when, in the most cliché choice possible, we read *Romeo and Juliet*. What newly minted teenage girl wouldn't want to listen to this young, pretty teacher, who might have herself been Juliet, wax poetic with her light lisp and lush eyebrows about requited but ill-fated adolescent love?

I left for college determined to deepen my relationship with the Bard; it, along with learning French (to complement the Spanish I already spoke), was one of my two goals for college. In class with my favourite English lit professor, John Bertolini, we examined Shakespeare's description of Cleopatra's regal procession into Rome, contrasting it with that same scene in Joseph Mankiewicz's 1963 film. In my junior year, I won my equivalent of the Miss Universe pageant when Professor Paul Cubeta selected me to join his exclusive ten-person advanced Shakespeare seminar. Many applied, few were chosen. The unlucky masses studied the Bard with him in a class of 25; we went to his home every Tuesday evening to sit on generously upholstered, well-worn furniture in his dimly lit drawing room. His wife baked lemon bars and other treats for us as both blood sugar boosters and rewards for the hours we spent poring over the texts. The comfy cushions belied a brutal academic rigour that only deepened my crush on Shakespeare.

"What, Ms. Meyer, do we make of Gertrude's reaction to Hamlet in the bedroom scene?" Professor Cubeta intoned, shrouded in scholarly gravitas.

I went mute in the spotlight, even though I'd read and pondered that—and every—scene over and over. Gertrude, in her anguish, told *me* that while she felt some guilt about her "o'er-hasty marriage" (II.ii.56-7), she did not know that Claudius killed Hamlet Sr., and that her son's erratic behaviour confounded and worried her. John Houseman as Harvard Law School Professor Kingsfield in *The Paper Chase* had nothing on Paul Cubeta, and my momentary hesitation gave him the opportunity to nullify me, his gaze turning to Tom, a nerd who seemed to know everything, making the humiliation complete. The shame rose in my cheeks, red enough to illuminate my dark corner of the lounge. I redoubled my efforts in reading *Macbeth* and all subsequent plays.

The year I graduated from college (1981), MetLife, the company for which both my father and I worked, sponsored an exhibit called *Shakespeare: The Globe and the World*, showcasing items from the Folger Shakespeare Library Collection. I felt like the once and future queen as we gained early access to the exhibit's stop at New York's American Museum of Natural History. The show's poster still looks over my shoulder in my office; I found the attendant coffee table book decades later in a charity bookshop in Stratford Upon Avon. I gobbled up the contents of that exhibition like so much porridge and mead, and watched my father glow with pride, knowing he had fed my fascination with the Elizabethan world.

I was left to my own devices to keep the Shakespark alive for much of my adult life. My father 'gently' guided me into the world of business and the pursuit of an MBA. "A degree in English," he advised, "is impractical. What are you going to do with that?" His parents had arrived at Ellis Island on separate ships bound from the same small town of Ioannina in north-western Greece. Neither of them completed more than a rudimentary elementary school education, if that. My grandfather (whom we called by the Greek "Papoo") cut and sold drop cloths in the Bronx. My grandparents survived the depression and valued education above all else, viewing it as their children's ticket to success in America. My father was the first in his family to graduate from high school and went on to take that honour for college (BA, Hunter College) and graduate school (MBA, Fairleigh Dickinson) as well. He worked at one company and one company only, starting as an underwriter at MetLife and rising through the ranks to become a Senior Vice President who developed several annuity and life insurance products, earned a seat in the executive dining room, and carried a key to the executive loo.

He was determined that I would have a better life than he—the typical immigrant and child-of-an-immigrant's dream. His fervour for me to succeed stemmed from a multi-headed Hydra: his Greek heritage and epoch valued men more than women; the American Dream dictated that each generation should surpass the previous one; he had no son, and so I became a surrogate heir for pressure to continue or magnify his success. He assigned me many conventionally male roles: cutting the grass, washing the car in the driveway, and learning to keep baseball scorebooks.

But that also meant I'd do it *his* way. When Middlebury College, my dream school, accepted me as a February Freshman (first semester in the spring, not the fall), they sent a course catalogue with the good news letter. Before I'd had a chance to thumb through it, he'd laid out my coursework for the next three and a half years, including how I'd make up the credits for the first semester and graduate "on time" with the rest of the fall freshman, rather than skiing the slopes of the Snow Bowl in cap and gown like the rest of the Febs. His plan did *not* include a major in English, but a more "practical" major in Economics. I thus spent my college career rationalising Supply and Demand in classes I excelled in but hated with my roommate Randy and most of the football team. At the same time, I managed to take almost as many courses in my preferred subjects: English and Hispanic literature, a dual minor.

When it came time for a career choice, my father again not-so-subtly shoehorned me into MetLife's management program as well as a night-time MBA at NYU (which I finished at Pepperdine University after accepting a new job in Los Angeles in 1984). I wanted to be a good girl and please my father, though I almost always felt that I'd fallen short. No matter what I did, it never seemed to elicit the accolades I'd hoped for. I could get five As and a B+ on a report card and we'd spend an hour discussing the disgraceful B. How, he urged, could "we" get it up for the next semester? The day I received my MA in Shakespeare Studies from the Shakespeare Institute, I could not help but wonder if he'd be proud.

My children either suffered or benefited from my Shakespeare obsession. I delighted in this captive audience with which to share my adoration, reasoning that early exposure minimises fear and resistance later. I'm proud that, as young adults, both are comfortably conversant in Shakespeak.

In 2011, like some jailbird pen pal desperate to keep in touch, I took it upon myself to embark upon a project called *The Shakespeare Diaries*. I committed to read or reread every single play and write essays on them "for fun," posting them to a WordPress site of the same name. "Having" to publish them, I reasoned, would provide pressure to write them.

"Why," people asked me, "in heaven's name would you voluntarily read every play and then write papers on them?"

"Love does funny things to people," I'd respond.

That endeavour took the better part of two years, and I experienced both elation and post-partum depression at having gestated and birthed this oeuvre. "Now what?" I thought, until a friend mentioned the UK-based master's programme in which her cousin had just enrolled.

I reacted much as others did to my reading marathon. "That's crazy. Why would I uproot a very comfortable life and take on a seemingly insurmountable challenge in a foreign country?"

As if on cue, my father's ghost stepped out of the shadows of my mind just like Hamlet's did, albeit with a different message. "Achieve," he said, instead of "Avenge." He waved Ganesh at me, vanquishing obstacles, my mother's ghost behind him, a vaporous Lady Macbeth, whispering, "I wish you'd start your life." I submitted applications to both KCL and the Shakespeare Institute. It felt like the most insane idea in the world, and the most natural.

My older son, Dustin, is as obsessed with Bob Dylan as I am with Shakespeare: he knows every track on every album by heart. He can recite lyrics, release dates, and live performances on demand (more than I can do for WS). Dustin, like I, has presented academic papers on his idol, and readily argues Dylan's merits, including his deserving the 2016 Nobel Prize in Literature. He likens Dylan's talent and influence to Shakespeare's. During a family wedding weekend in the Catskills, we made our own pilgrimage to Big Pink, an aptly named Pepto-Bismol-coloured house where Dylan and The Band recorded what would become both *The Basement Tapes* and *Music from Big Pink*.

What do we hope to glean from walking in our idols' footsteps or viewing and even touching relics associated with them? Pilgrimages, official and unofficial, abound. Loyal followers flock to Jerusalem, Graceland, and Stratford Upon Avon alike. There is something in simply making the effort to get to Mecca (wherever that is for each acolyte) that represents a certain level of devotion. The trip itself is evidence of faith.

A special set of obsessives takes it a step further. Certain Christians venerate pieces of the Cross as certain Shakespeare enthusiasts exalt shards of his backyard Mulberry tree. The practices defy rationality: if every piece of *the* Cross and *the* Mulberry tree were genuine, the lumber would require all the trees from both the New and Nottingham Forests. These places and relics have intrinsic value as tangible representations of history. I read and saw Shakespeare plays for years, but on my first visit to Stratford Upon Avon, during a visit to England with my mother in the early 1980s, I stood at the Gower Memorial at the foot of the Clopton Bridge, dizzily feeling the urge to genuflect. Decades later, when I crossed the floor at Hall's Croft where Shakespeare's daughter and son-in-law lived, the tour guide assured us that the man himself trod the same stones during visits. I stood still in the worn depression of one stone and closed my eyes. The energy radiated up from that surface into my body and I felt as possessed as I did later at my seat by his grave. Proximity makes the deity more real.

This holds true for more personal items as well. We all hold on to things that have little intrinsic but immense sentimental meaning. I wonder how my Greek and Russian forebears decided what to bring with them en route to the New World.

I see the Russian samovar as a kind of genie's lamp: my maternal relatives' essences could all be in that tea urn waiting for me to rub the side and release them (which, perhaps, I do in prose). The canes my father collected over a lifetime stand sentry in an umbrella holder at my front door. I remember the provenance of each. My Papoo's amber worry beads hang on my bedroom doorknob.

The collected relics are reminders and receptacles: talismans with which we surround ourselves because they represent something we love. The closer they are to the era and/or person, the more cherished they are, as if, in an eschatological calculus equation, we know we can approach the person but never ever actually get there. These items minimise the area under the curve. No one who owns a purported moon rock has any illusions that they themselves walked on the surface of our satellite, but touching it is the next best thing.

Shakespeare wasn't always *all that*. In fact, many of his peers disparaged him. Ben Jonson, who later sang his praises in the *First Folio*, said Shakespeare had "small Latin and less Greek," implying his education was inferior to that of his more erudite colleagues and competitors. Robert Greene, Master of the Revels (like an FCC censor), famously called him an "upstart crow," implying that he plagiarised others' work.

Not until a group of his friends and business associates posthumously compiled all his extant work in the *First Folio*—viewed by many as the most important secular book in the English language—could anyone even purchase all his works. During the late-fifteenth-century dawn of printing, paper and the process were costly. Librarians chained books by their leather bindings to the shelves of the Bodleian Library at Oxford because, as a guide told me, they "cost about what a sports car would cost today." Most people had only the Bible at home.

Had Hemmings and Condell not published the *First Folio* in 1623, there'd be no Bardolatry, no Shakespeare Institute, no pilgrimages nor attendant memoirs.

Shakespeare came from humble beginnings in that now-famous house on Henley Street. His father, John, had a licence to make and sell gloves from a room on the street level. John had no such dispensation to trade sheep wool or lend money, but did so anyway, and eventually landed crosswise with the law. Also, it was rumoured that he was Catholic, which was frowned upon in the days just after the reign of King Henry VIII, who broke up with Rome's flagship Christianity in favour of his own homegrown brand, The Church of England. These transgressions prevented John Shakespeare from attaining a much-coveted family crest until his son achieved a measure of success in Londontown.

As a playwright for and stakeholder in the King's Men, one of Queen Elizabeth I's sanctioned acting companies, Shakespeare made a name for himself in the London theatre community and enough money to return to Stratford Upon Avon as a local-boy-done-good. As such, he bought his father a family crest and himself the second-largest home in town. (Alas, it no longer stands. The post-Shakespeare owner, incensed by tourists gaping in the windows and pilfering pieces of the Mulberry tree, had it demolished.)

But he was no Lin-Manuel Miranda. Without today's 24/7 technology-enabled news cycle, it's unlikely that folks in far-flung Liverpool or York even knew his name.

Even after the *First Folio*, Shakespeare didn't attain legendary status until David Garrick, a London-based Shakespearean actor, devised and executed a plan to hold a Jubilee in Shakespeare's honour in Stratford Upon Avon in 1769. Given the poor planning, high expectations, insufficient accommodations, and torrential rain, it's a wonder that Garrick pulled off this Early Modern Woodstock. Yet the statue for which he raised funds has recently been refurbished and replaced in the alcove in which it has watched over Sheep Street since the Jubilee, rechristened in festivities overseen by no less than Dame Judi Dench and Sir Kenneth Branagh.

The reverence continued to grow in the Victorian Era. The romanticists (Wordsworth, Shelley, Keats, Blake, Byron) adulated him, contributing to his popularity. Keats is said to have carried a miniature portrait of the Bard with him.

This, combined with easier travel between England and the continent and easier access to theatre and print books, started the steroidisation of Shakespeare, the man, into Shakespeare, the legend.

Now, when people from around the world are asked to name the most readily identifiable English cultural icon, it's as often Shakespeare as it is the late Queen. He sits centre stage at British Olympics opening ceremonies and appears in various guises on countless souvenirs. Considered the best and most important writer in the English language, he has achieved superstar status in academia, the arts, and the tourist trade. I often imagine him reposing below the floor of Holy Trinity Church, not rolling in his grave, but shaking his head and chuckling: *Much Ado About Nothing.*

Stratford presented an opportunity to explore and a challenge to my personal Bard worship. I embarked on the odyssey with as much trepidation as anticipation. The memory of the hamlet from my honeymoon 26 years earlier was hazy. I could hardly wait to immerse myself in the big Shakesfest, but I worried that the reality might fail to live up to the hype in my mind. I also wondered if I would prove a worthy pilgrim.

SUA is ground zero for Shakespeople. As such, it embodies both the apogee and nadir of the adulation; the sublime and the ridiculous stand side by side. The Shakespeare Institute, Shakespeare Birthplace Trust, and Royal Shakespeare Company (RSC) house some of the most erudite minds in the Shakesverse, and churn out research, publications, and performances like so much goat's milk from his mother Mary Arden's nearby farm. However, as with any form of worship, opportunists and parasites sense and exploit opportunities for material gain. In Disney-like gift shops, vendors sell his image on everything: keychains, T-shirts, mugs, and more, often misquoting him or attributing words to him that he never, as far as we know, said. Streets, rowboats for hire, and menu items are named for his plays. I regularly saw busloads of tourists flock to Henley Street to take selfies in front of The Birthplace, never going inside. The newest statue at the base of Henley Street resembles John Malkovich more than any image of Shakespeare I've ever seen and is more nausea- than reverence-inducing. A barge moored near the RSC sells Shakespeare ice cream, while a shop in town offers Shakespeare Gin, another Shakesbeer.

The epitome of this coexistent contradiction comes in the form of the laudatory birthday parade, which snakes through the streets of town every April 23. Literati from the three venerated institutions as well as dignitaries from around the world come out in full regalia and march with military solemnity. Schoolchildren do the same, clad in uniform, carrying traditional yellow flowers to place at his grave. On a stand erected just in front of what used to be the town market hall (now a Barclays Bank branch), the mayor and an emcee welcome well-wishers by the thousands, and eventually an actor who resembles the Bard all but jumps out of a birthday cake to bequeath the mayor a quill pen to place in the right hand of the Bard's bust at the grave. Morris dancers dance, costumed characters carouse, vendors sell food and merchandise, fun is had by all. It feels very much like a Main Street Disney parade.

Ultimately for me, though, he merited my idolatry, and I proved up to the challenge of idolising him. I longed to get closer to the object of my adoration—to see if his glitter was gold and not pyrite, and in immersing myself in his world, both physically and literally, I felt fulfilled, not disappointed. I loved being on the "inside"—being a resident and not a visitor. I swept into Holy Trinity to sit with him without having to pay because I lived in the CV37. I had access to the bowels of the SBT where the *Folio*, the *Holinshed's Chronicles*, and other true treasures lived behind ten-inch locked steel doors in humidity- and temperature-controlled silence. I walked up and down the shores of the Avon, where he would have walked, and admired the swans for whom he is nicknamed. I ate and drank and breathed it all in, feeling like I was getting a direct infusion of Shakesblood all year long.

And in return, I gave him my all. I attended every class, play, lecture, and event that the town offered. I scoured sacred volumes in the libraries to deepen my understanding of his world and his work. I sat with some of the best Shakespeare academics on the planet and just let their knowledge osmose into me. I went beyond the absurd surface of the Bardolatry to the sublime interior of his world.

<u>Shakesfest</u>

The overwhelming sense of perpetual celebration of his existence that Shakespeare nerds feel.

Chapter 4:

The Mature Student
(on learning later in life)

"What is your study?"

King Lear (III.iv.88)

"You have to narrow that a bit," chuckled Mr. Warren in a coup of understatement when I told him I wanted to write about World War II. My ninth-grade World History teacher and I were meeting to discuss a topic for my first-ever research paper. He knew that WWII's many years, battlefields, airspaces, and socioeconomic geopolitical nuances would not fit snugly into the assignment's prescribed ten handwritten (this was, after all, 1973) pages. Like a bomber on a midnight sortie, I zeroed in on the target of The Battle of the Bulge, and even found a primary source. The father of a toddler for whom I babysat fought in that five-week skirmish, and with eyes downcast under a cloud of PTSD, he mumbled, "It was cold. It was dark. It was scary as hell." I got an A+ on the paper.

"You have to narrow that a bit," wrote my dissertation advisor in an email when I'd suggested the following topic for my Ph.D. in Holistic Nutrition: *With So Much Information Out*

There About Nutrition and its Impact on Health, Why Do People Continue to Make Such Poor Choices? Like a lab technician examining a pathogen under a 1500x magnification microscope, I focused my lens of analysis on the validity, accuracy, and utility of ten years' worth of nutrition articles in mainstream magazines. The review panel awarded me an A on the treatise in which I concluded that most of what we read is confusing, unsubstantiated, unhelpful drivel.

"No," said my dissertation advisor, Dr. Martin Wiggins, when I, folded into the cluttered couch in his claustrophobic aerie of an office, told him that I wanted to write on the significance of the number three (my favourite) in Shakespeare's plays. He knew the topic was too vast, unwieldy, and vague to wrangle into a 15,000-word master's thesis, and he used about that many to explain why. I hung on every one, as I did on all the pearls of wisdom that dripped from his treasure trove of a brain. With his help, and after several false starts, I homed in—like the hawkeyed splendid birds of prey I watched show off at the nearby Warwick Castle—on exploring Shakespeare's non-expository opening scenes to illustrate the scenes' intrinsic value.

I prided myself on being an excellent student and had the external accolades to prove it: enshrinement in Edison Junior High School's *Book of Emerald*, awards in several subjects in high school, magna cum laude and Phi Beta Kappa at Middlebury, and a 4.0 GPA at Pepperdine (MBA). But Cerberus, sporting the heads of my father's ghost, my impostor syndrome, and my own unrealistically high expectations, had often been my fang-toothed companion. Now, that tri-headed dog stood snarling at the entrance to the Shakespeare Institute.

I felt intense pressure to produce something of value that I could wave as a banner of success, particularly after devoting nearly a third of my life to raising my boys full-time. No matter how often the media assigned an astronomical price tag on a stay-at-home mother's contribution to the household,

I never felt valued for the essential and important work I did. My ex-husband's colleagues' eyes would glaze over when I met them at company holiday parties; they'd met so many identical soccer moms who added nothing to the conversation or the world as far as they were concerned. Only on the rare occasion when I bothered to open my mouth and eloquently and intelligently opine on the topic at hand did their heads swivel to see me anew. "The Stepford Wife is a *real* girl with a *brain*!" I could hear them think as loudly as if they'd shouted it across the festive table.

If being a "housewife" made me transparent, being a *divorced* one made me invisible. There is no seat at the table for a singleton at the weekend dinners to which I used to get invited as part of a couple. I'm not sure that I did this consciously, but all my achievements, both intellectual and physical (a black belt in Tae Kwon Do, a Yoga Teach Certification, Reiki Mastership, a Ph.D. in Holistic Nutrition, and the *Shakespeare Diaries* project), were no doubt a cry to be seen and heard in a suburb and larger world that perceived me as nothing more than a cut-out in a chain of one-dimensional paper dolls.

Although I had already completed two graduate degrees, I had not submitted a literary essay for grading since graduating college 36 years prior. Most of my new classmates had graduated mere months before. Although we shared a common language, I had no idea if or how much the UK academic system and expectations might differ from those to which I'd become accustomed at home.

Per usual, I prepared like a Boy Scout. Lecturers seemed pleasantly surprised that I'd read not only every word of every assigned text, but also each of the half dozen or so items on the "suggested outside reading" list; classmates chided me. I underlined; I annotated. I had already read every play at least once, but had steered clear of the Sonnets, which scared me. Poetry's lined, rhymed, metered language intimidated me—it seemed designed to obfuscate its subjects, exclude me from the party, and leave me feeling stupid. In those halcyon days after I arrived in England, but before the course started, I read all 154.

My preparation also included pirouetting through The Works, a packed-to-the-gills book/stationery/souvenir shop, like a happy parent in a Staples back-to-school commercial, stocking up on blue pens, notebooks, and A4 pads of paper. The virginal white, orderly ruled pages held such potential. I hoped that highlighters and sticky notes coordinated with coloured pens and pencils would help me magically transform the jumbled thoughts I'd no doubt have during assignments into clearly delineated theses on the page.

The small, white corner console in my small, white, cottage cheese-walled Old Town flat in College Mews was meant to hold a television. No frivolous entertainment for me, I decreed, believing I had to burn the midnight academic oil for the duration of this scholastic sojourn. I had no television, no cable, and no television licence. That low, triangular piece of furniture became a shrine to the academic year. A small bust of Shakespeare presided over the stationery and books, which would multiply like rabbits over the next thirteen months.

My college-level and later independent studies amounted to playing on a Double-A baseball team in Iowa compared to the Major League diamond into which I was about to dig my cleats. The Shakespeare Institute is *The Show* of Bardcentric studies.

The baseball analogy seems particularly apt because, when I was 12, my father taught me the intricacies of scorekeeping: a skill that I put to good use for that Edison Junior High School team, where my boyfriend argued every time I credited a fielder with an error rather than him with a hit. As the years went on and my resentment of my father's controlling nature and insatiable standards grew, baseball held our relationship together like the red threads on the ball or the rawhide laces on a mitt. When I lived in Los Angeles and my parents were still in New York, we spent hours on the phone during the Mets' 1986 World Series against the Red Sox, when long-distance calls cost more than tickets to Shea Stadium. We cheered and shouted and cried at Bill Buckner's error in game six and the Amazins' comeback win in game seven to clinch the title. We came as close to hugging each other as we could from 3,000 miles away.

The Shakespeare Institute faculty serve as the seasoned managers that know how to get the best performance from every player. Collectively, they intimidated me as much as my dearth of relevant academic experience. Like a pair of yin-yang coaches of winning National League and American League teams, the two elder Shakesmen, Doctors John Jowett and Martin Wiggins had very different focuses and styles. Both would impart their knowledge freely and mentor me caringly in my fledgling struggle to keep up with my cohort and to prove that I deserved the place they had granted me in the Institute.

John served both as lecturer in Textual Studies and Research Skills and as my personal tutor. He wrote the definitive *Shakespeare and Text* and co-edited the biblical *New Oxford Shakespeare: The Complete Works Modern Critical Edition.* The former stands as the seminal reference for Shakespearean textual studies, following a trail of sometimes very obscure breadcrumbs on the path to understanding how Shakespeare's words made it from his quill pen to the various printed iterations. In examining that complex and often clouded sequence, he discusses everything from the "foul papers," the original drafts, to "cue scripts," the copies used by actors in the theatres (which, to save on printing costs and to prevent actors selling their copies to competing playwrights, contained only that actor's lines), to the evolution of printing and publishing that made versions of Shakespeare's work available to the public. The *New Oxford Shakespeare* is one of the most definitive and comprehensive compendiums of all of Shakespeare's works, including copious commentary and context for each.

"Oxford" couldn't be more apt; those were the only shirts and shoes John wore. Plaid blazer-clad, he might have stepped out of a Brooks Brothers catalogue, or central casting for a prototypical university professor. His silver wire-rimmed glasses only honed his already razor-sharp focus on his subject. His demure and introverted demeanour belied his deep commitment to students and quiet sense of humour. Students who skipped the weekly Friday football game on the pitch behind the Institute and the post-game drinks in the West End Pub (the Westy) afterwards (where he'd enjoy a pint of Timothy Taylor and always stand a round for the sweaty, exhausted participants) saw only one side of this genuine gentleman. Though an Olympic torchbearer of all things Bard, I sensed he felt most at home on that field kicking a ball into the net or hiking in some remote brae in Scotland or Wales with his wife Sarah.

His counterpart, Martin Wiggins, was responsible for what we affectionately referred to as "The Wiggalogue": *British Drama 1533-1642: A Catalogue.* This series, his life's work, will eventually stretch to twelve volumes and provide an exhaustive reference for every piece of English, Scottish, Welsh, and Irish drama written over the eleven-decade interval between the English Reformation and the English Revolution.

When I asked Martin if he had an intricate schema for the myriad facts that he'd collected and curated over the years pasted on some wall like a forensic CSI detective's case chart, he simply tapped his head and said, "It's all in here." The Institute's very own Man in Black (his actual nickname, based on his stringently monochromatic wardrobe), Martin's *Back to the Future* Doc Brown hairdo provided evidence that he devoted nearly 100% of his vast brain capacity to scholarship and not grooming. But his hueless attire belied his colourful personality. Martin coordinated the wildly popular weekly Thursday night and summertime multi-week play reading marathons, reciting his parts with verve and appropriate accents, delighting all.

Slightly obsessed with cats, he would squeeze a small toy cat that mewed loudly whenever one was mentioned in an Early Modern play. Each reader hoped that the master might miss a feline reference so we could point it out with the eagerness of a *Jeopardy!* participant working the buzzer. His sense of humour was as bawdy as Shakespeare's, his knowledge vast, his patience for serious students infinite, and his tolerance for fools low.

Martin and John's combined brainpower could have lit Warwickshire for a year. It certainly illuminated my world. My reverence and respect for them was and is as vast and deep as the Atlantic that I'd crossed to learn at their feet.

I could hardly believe my luck at landing in a place where much of the world's Shakespeare braintrust not only taught and researched, but generously imparted that knowledge to those of us privileged enough to share the space. The building itself was originally a home (of novelist Marie Corelli, Stratford's other prodigal literary offspring), so its structure leant itself to frequent, casual interaction with all the faculty. No sprawling campus, this—John or Martin were as likely to be sipping tea in the conservatory as any of us students.

We convened religiously for Thursday afternoon lectures to welcome Shakespeare academics from the Institute, the RSC, and the Birthplace Trust as well as other visiting experts, actors, and even an MP. Unlike any of the other places I might have studied, including KCL (which rejected me because they did not feel that I "could adequately cope with the programme's academic rigour"), this place at this moment in time allowed me to bathe in the highest level of Shakespeare knowledge, 24/7. I could almost have learned just by osmosis alone, but the fact is I had to *work*. This exhilarated and terrified me. I had the world of Shakespeare at my fingertips; how could I prove myself worthy?

When I told friends and family what I planned for the year, they supported me, but most looked at me askance. "The last thing I would ever do is go back to school. Intentionally. Voluntarily. All that work..." Indeed, why choose to work so hard? Why work at all? Why did Shakespeare toil so; why does anyone? These questions crossed my mind as I crossed the ocean. Theoretically, I could retire. I could do *no* work, but somehow that felt like sloth; like laziness; like disappointing my father and myself.

Great thinkers and writers have gone to great lengths to evaluate, value, and validate *work*. Their notions help frame how we—how I—think about it. Aristotle and Plato valued "craft-driven productive activity," but they also stressed the importance of leisure as an essential element of the virtuous life. In his *Republic*, Plato acknowledged "the centrality of work to social and personal life." Confucius lauded hard work and perseverance for its own sake. Christianity saw work as divine—a way to glorify God and embody his will. Marx focused on those who perform the exertion and decried the alienation and exploitation of the working class. Capitalists, he claimed, pocketed the value created from labourers' blood, sweat, and tears, while the labourers' compensation was little more than those profusions. In *Civilization and its Discontents*, Freud noted that "man needs two things for happiness: Love and work, work and love."

These thinkers—disparate in time and place—all felt that effort merited their effort. On the surface, they examined it from different perspectives: socioeconomic, political, spiritual, and psychological. They esteemed it for different reasons: for having intrinsic value, for creating balance, for cultivating piety, for contributing to society. Yet, below the surface, they share the notion that work in and of itself creates meaning and value. This lofty thinking about work seems to imply that work imbues life with meaning, and conversely, that without effort life is naught but Macbeth's "brief candle."

I thought of my grandfathers. Even at a young age, I felt hard-pressed to believe that their jobs were anything more than a means to an end. David, my mother's curmudgeonly father, was a glazer in Union City, New Jersey. My paternal grand-father Saul produced drop cloths in the Bronx. I doubt that either had time to pursue self-actualisation, especially given the mere glimpses that I got of the physical and financial struggles their vocations involved. However, both men were observant Orthodox Jews. I attended their shuls, usually for the High Holy Days—the former's in Lakewood, NJ, the latter's near Fordham Road in the Bronx. They both dovened, yarmulked, and tallited solemnly. They admonished my sister and me severely if we giggled during the services we dreaded attending. Maybe this spirituality imbued their lives with significance beyond that granted by their vocations.

Abraham Maslow helped me to further understand this drive to exert myself with his triangular "hierarchy of needs." He recognised why most of us work at all: to fulfil the most basic physiological needs of food and shelter. But at the pinnacle of the mountain—the place that most motivated me—lies "self-actualisation": the work we do, most often in our minds, that we *choose* more than are *compelled* to do. It is the work that allows us to maximise our potential. While a physical task may satisfy the more rarefied air in the triangle's pinnacle—climbing Mount Everest, for example—it is most often more cerebral. The trite, often bandied-about maxim, "If you do what you love you'll never work a day in your life," attributed to everyone from Mark Antony to Confucius to Mark Twain, sums it up well for me and helps me understand why, in a quest for purpose, I chose to sign up for, rather than shy away from, more work.

I worked far harder on this course than I had at anything else, except perhaps during my own personal labour days giving birth to two boys. That, though, clearly fell into the physical category, while this would tax me mentally, drain me emotionally, and exhaust me physically. Earning an MA in Shakespeare Studies from the University of Birmingham's Shakespeare Institute would be *my* Mount Everest.

I roamed all over Stratford Upon Avon, peripatetic in my work habits. I sat in my flat on a white chair at the round white table. I sat downstairs at the RSC Café so I could see the river. I sat upstairs at the RSC Café so I couldn't. I sat in the seat by the window at Caffe Nero so I could see the tourists traipse up and down Henley Street. I sat upstairs at Caffe Nero so I couldn't. I sat at the street-side Swan Café so I could wrap myself in the warm wood panelling and see nothing else but my books. I sat in the Warwickshire Public Library in an Elizabethan building refurbished courtesy of an Andrew Carnegie donation. I sat at Boston Tea Party so I could eat while pretending to work.

And, of course, I sat in the cramped and crowded Shakespeare Institute library, especially if I needed access to reference material. While much of it has been digitised, much remains concealed within embossed leather-bound volumes dating almost as far back as the Bard himself. We could not remove these rare, unique treasures from the premises, so if we needed them, we were de facto prisoners of the oddly configured space that Marie Corelli never intended for use as a research library.

I didn't want to get sent back down to the minors. My work

needed to reflect my high level of respect for my tutors, so I agonised over each essay. I researched my topics, gathering references from the plays and background material to cover every possible angle. I read primary sources and centuries of Shakespeare criticism so complex that I often struggled just to make sense of it. And of course, when I thought I'd looked at everything, a professor—Martin, usually, whom I'd believed had memorised not only everything Shakespeare had ever written but also every volume in that library—would offhandedly ask, "But surely, Diane, you've looked at..." Erasmus? Topsell? Alciato? Or some other obscure genius who had written something essential to my topic. "Not yet," I'd say, feeling defeated and glum but trying to sound engaged and cheerful, "but I'm on my way to the library now," as I trudged back in that direction.

Sometimes I would keep researching because it meant I didn't have to start writing. Mounds of notes accrued, like grocery bags full of ingredients heaped on the counter, waiting to become a gourmet meal with nary a cookbook or recipe in sight. I'd shuffle the pages around. I'd code notes I'd already made with those colourful highlighters. I'd mince and chop and season the olio in my mind and then on the paper like the *Macbeth* witches stirring their cauldron, hoping for magic.

The days leading up to the end of the first term in December grew shorter as my academic to-do list grew longer. The sun would begin its descent behind the Old Town rooftops where mourning doves huddled to share warmth at 16:00. It was cold. I was cold. I had a cold. The triad of essays that I needed to complete would comprise a post-holiday corpus, my first efforts at serious Shakespeare scholarship.

The festive and fantastical Shakespeare Institute holiday fete faded into memory. The friends with whom I'd exchanged gifts and toasted the holidays in ugly Christmas jumpers that we'd bought together for £5 at the Saturday town market scattered to far-flung corners of the British Isles to cosy in and celebrate with their families.

I got bronchitis—and steroids and an inhaler to deal with it—from my GP at the Arden Medical Centre. My energy level was low, my anxiety level high. Those few of us still in SUA spent all our waking hours in the Institute library in a desperate sprint to hunt down and retrieve source material. We either had to take notes furiously or spend a small fortune to copy the pages we needed—or might need. The library closed for about three weeks for the holidays and would not reopen until the beginning of the second term, just prior to our essays' due date. Handing in essays late or in excess of the 5,000-word limit resulted in grade penalisation, so we had to get any research we needed from the library before the doors shut for break.

These circumstances, in the best of times, would have stressed the coolest of customers. But this was, in a very Dickensian sense of the word, the worst of times. The boiler in the library failed just before break began. Since the holidays were nigh, and the Shakespeare Institute—the poor neglected stepchild of the University of Birmingham—sat forty miles south of the main campus, they wouldn't send a technician. Our multi-talented caretaker, David, tried to tinker with the petulant machine. Initially I believed this imminently kind, reclusively quiet, and somewhat dishevelled blue khaki-clad man lived at the Institute. He was there long before any of us arrived and was there no matter how late we stayed. I only realised he lived quite close to me in Old Town when I saw him cycling to work just ahead of me during my morning walk to class one day. He took care of everything physical at the Institute, from tending to the lovely back garden, to setting up for Thursday lectures and its following tea reception in the lecture hall and conservatory, to dealing with pesky boilers.

But this Jack of all Trades was no match for the beastly boiler. He acquiesced and finally called in professionals. Several of us watched a pair of repairmen convene in the boiler closet and come out shaking their heads in defeat. They had to, they told David as we shivered nearby, order parts that would not arrive until the new year.

Six or so of us sat at a wide bank of tables to the left of the entrance, four chairs on each side facing each other. The monitors at each seat hid our desperation from those across from us as we typed frantically in fingerless gloves, our breath visible vapour.

"If this were the States, a dozen helicopter parents would have hovered over Old Joe (the University of Birmingham's clocktower, its most recognisable landmark) with megaphones threatening lawsuits if they didn't immediately provide their precious offspring with heat," I said to no one in particular and everyone within earshot. Here, though, they took the most famous national maxim very seriously. We were meant to *keep calm and carry on*: we all donned extra mufflers and lap blankets, and vaguely trusted that "someone would get the heat back on at some point." I shivered and tried not to cry as I wrapped my Edinburgh Woollen Mill Black Watch Plaid cape more tightly around my shoulders.

With slightly blue fingertips, I typed out an email to the provost in Birmingham, outlining the situation, noting that the conditions bordered on dangerous for students and staff alike. The next morning, back for another round of *Beat the Clock*, I watched David shuffle in with space heaters that he placed around our tables and the staff desks. I opened my email to read a genuinely concerned response from said Provost.

"Ms. Lowman," he intoned, "I was entirely unaware of the dire situation at the Institute library. Thank you for bringing it to my attention. I will look into it with the aim of restoring the heat as soon as possible."

I marvelled that no one in Stratford had thought to contact

the mothership. While Santa wouldn't make it in time with either boiler parts *or* coal, at least we had a modicum of warmth.

But when those doors locked for the last time in 2017, so even Karin (head librarian), Kate, and Anne (her assistants) could go home, I felt like Dr. Frank Poole on Discovery One in *2001: A Space Odyssey*. A sharp pair of umbilical scissors cut the cord, and I, a novice astronaut, hurtled into space. Dark matter engulfed me and filled the space between my ears, and out of that void I needed to create three 5,000-word essays in three weeks, which would determine my entire grade for each of the three courses which I'd just completed.

From Christmas Eve Day through Boxing Day (December 26), the only space in which I might work was my 400 square foot flat. I could no longer roam in search of inspiration and optimal conditions. My round white table doubled as a dining surface and desk. Now it looked like an operating theatre in a MASH (Mobile Army Surgical Hospital) unit: piles of books and papers marked with colourful Post-It tabs lay strewn about, waiting for me to make them whole in a cohesive treatise. I had to focus on one essay at a time, so the spectres of the two others hovered in the corner like patients in an ER triage area. They needed attention, too, but they'd have to wait until the critical mess on the table coalesced. The triad would comprise a post-holiday corpus, my first efforts at serious Shakespeare scholarship.

I felt the pressing sense of urgency of a military medic, but since the patient was not yet exactly bleeding out on the table, I managed to hone the art of procrastination as sharply as any scalpel. Henry the Hoover—the red canister vacuum with a smiley face who lived in my utility closet—saw more action in the three weeks before I had to hand in the essays than he had in the last three months. My carpets had never been so clean. My cuticles, too, received an inordinate amount of attention. I rearranged the Spartan items of clothing sitting and hanging in my tiny bedroom closet so much that I could sense their irritation and desire to be left alone in the dark. All the while, I felt guilty, knowing I should plant my bum in the uncomfortable white wooden chair that I'd tried to make more ergonomic with a cheap seat cushion from Poundland. The books and I had stare-offs, like the ones my college roommate and I had with our calculus texts on the top floor of the Milliken residence hall at Middlebury. The notes called me, sirens from the island of Academia; I resisted but could not plug my ears and restrain myself like Odysseus did—I had to heed their call. The essays would not write themselves.

When I finally crawled into bed each night, a chorus of voices of uncertainty serenaded me. Was what I'd scribbled that day adequate? Had I left anything out? Did any of it make any sense? I wondered how I would manage to create a creme brulee of the ingredients swirling in my brain for the next section I needed to write. I dreamt about scenes, citations, and pages slashed with the red ink of criticism. Sometimes my mind worked while I slept, and I woke up with a clear vision for the next section. Sometimes it, too, slept, and I woke up feeling heavy with uncertainty under my white duvet cover, knit-covered hot water bottle still on my feet to keep them warm.

The constant gnawing feeling that I should be writing when I did *anything* else waned once I acquiesced and shifted my brain from neutral into drive. When I could grasp the threads that I'd gathered and began, I could write with the same fluidity with which I knit. I did that often back home, ostensibly to keep myself from snacking at night, and to keep my mind from wandering into dark places. I knit so much that every neck I knew was bedecked with a homemade muffler. It had got to the point where I was handing them out to near strangers. I'd put down the needles and left them behind in favour of the pen. When I managed to land in the *zone*, I could see the whole shawl: colours, patterns, sizes all seemed so obvious to me. When I knit at home, I didn't even look at the needles or the yarn—I worked on autopilot, counting stitch-es and creating patterns in my head. When the ink flowed (I always wrote longhand first; typing it all in on my MacBook allowed me to make initial edits) in Stratford, like the water in the nearby Avon over Lucy's Mill, I wrote, too, almost with-out thinking. It was as if my brain had stealthily developed the argument while Henry hummed over the oatmeal carpet. I would write and write and write until my hand cramped, teapots full of PG Tips fuelling me with caffeine and comfort. In England, the answer to stressors large and small is always, "I'll put the kettle on." I would vomit out volumes until my vision blurred.

"I can't see anymore. I can't think anymore. I'm not certain that I'm even writing in intelligible English anymore. I can't do this," I whined to Dustin one dark day at dusk after a few hours of spewing onto the page.

"I get it. I do. Just stop for now. Put it away. But remember, Mom, you did sign up for this. I mean, this is voluntary."

I could hardly celebrate after I'd drafted the first essay. I'd only finished the first leg of the triathlon. And even after complet-ing the rest of the race, there'd be no flopping prostrate on the ground or onlookers to shower me in champagne; I'd have to analyse my own performance. I wouldn't push "submit" until I'd thoroughly reviewed each of the three essays for coherence and compliance with the MLA academic format. It was as if I'd had one of three impacted wisdom teeth pulled and had to go back to the oral surgeon two more times within the same three weeks, knowing full well the suffering that lay in store for me.

By the time I did hit "submit," the holidays, including an uneventful New Year's Eve, faded in the rear-view mirror and a new term dawned. Friends returned, and we toasted our accomplishments at the West End. Cooper, the big Great Dane who lived there, came close. We knew each other well by then, but he didn't know how much more he weighed than I. He let me scratch under his chin; I knew he preferred that to having his ears rubbed. He leaned into me as he relaxed; as he leaned into me, I relaxed. Only then did I realise how thoroughly the essays had exhausted me mentally and physically, and he must have sensed it. He stood stone still and silent and just let my stress pour out as I poured a pint of Guinness down my gullet. He may not have been a therapy dog, but he was mine at that moment.

Since the grade for each class depended entirely on these final 5,000-word essays, my normal modus operandi did not serve me. I was that annoying student who read everything, and always had something to say in every class (except calculus)—the cliché, hand raised, arm straining, almost lifting out of my seat, "Ooh! Ooh!" I studied for each quiz and test in all my other academic lives as if one subtracted point would equal failure. Here, there were no quizzes, no tests, no credit for in-class presentations or enthusiastic participation—or even for showing up.

Credit or not, I doubled down on those efforts, because this was not just something to do after undergrad and before entering the workforce. Nor was it a carefully coordinated next step on the path to a career in academia. I was too *mature* for either of those. It was the balm to my itchy midlife crisis; a waking dream for which I'd given up every vestige of an ostensibly comfortable and secure existence.

I wrote my essay for Early Modern Playhouse Practices on *The Music of the Spheres*. That theory, originating in ancient Greece and expanded upon during the Renaissance, associated the alignment of celestial orbs with music. Many of Shakespeare's plays make reference to this philosophical concept of *musica universalis* and I chose to research and explain those.

Two seemingly disparate catalysts motivated my choice. First, during a period of low intellectual stimulation when my children were young, I delved deeply into outer space. I read everything Stephen Hawking and Brian Greene wrote and found superstring theory music to my ears. While I did not pretend to understand the mathematics behind it, its conclusion—that the entire universe boiled down to vibrational musical notes—made almost mystical sense to me. Second, Pete Townshend whispered in my ear when he wrote "there once was a note," in his song *Pure and Easy*. That note, he said, was "eternal." For me, this was so meta: a song, written way before the advent of superstring theory, intuiting musical notes' existence and import.

Naive old American grad student that I was, I opened my paper on *The Music of the Spheres* in Shakespeare with references to physics and rock 'n' roll. In fact, I started the essay by quoting Pete Townshend. I thought I was so clever, tying all these literary, cultural, and scientific threads together. Poor Simon Smith. The slight class lecturer with slightly avian features was a genuinely brilliant man and delightful human. "The scholarship in this essay is quite adequate." He sat at his desk across from me in an office he shared with another faculty member. "In advanced academia, however, it is best to omit generalised references to authors and subjects you do not intend to fully research and cite in a 5,000-word essay. Better to thoroughly explore the subject at hand." He looked up then, too Britishly polite before to meet my eyes as he explained the rules of the game. I got it: Stick to Shakespeare, not astrophysics, not The Who. I thought I was such a rock star having invoked a rock star to talk about the Bard (who, of course, I idolised as a rock star). Really, it was more *A Comedy of Errors*.

Martin also had to put me in my place. In a paper on *Cori-*

olanus, I'd referred to the female characters, whose names all begin with V, as "The Vagina Monologues" and "The V Squad."

"Diane," he said, imbuing my first name with the gravity of an eleventh commandment, "you have not yet earned the right to quip."

"Isn't there any place for humour in Shakespearean scholarship?" I asked.

"I have earned that right. You have not...no matter how clever the moniker."

I was chastened, yes, but I completely understood (and he did think it was amusing). These mentors were teaching me not only about Shakespeare, but how to write seriously and academically about him.

I sat with John in the "Westy" one evening after a Friday football game. He had awarded me the highest grade possible on my essay on *The Foul Papers*. In it, I made an apparently cogent argument for their existence (academics do not all agree).

"You know you did quite well on that paper," he said, Timothy Taylor pint in hand.

"Thank you. I worked really hard on it," I told him. "I never had confidence in what I produce here. It's so daunting."

"Your comments are always insightful. Sometimes I think you might be the only student who has read that whole book in years. Why would you feel that way?" He seemed genuinely curious.

"I'm old. I'm out of practice. I'm American. Did I ever tell you what KCL said in rejecting my application to their programme?"

"No, what did they say?"

"It seemed they'd forgotten to even respond to my application. I followed up with them and got a curt email saying: 'We regret to inform you that we have denied you admittance to

King's College London's Masters of Arts Course in Shakespeare Studies because we do not believe you are qualified to meet the rigours of the academic challenges of the programme.'"

"Really?" John just laughed out loud, shook his head, and had another sip of his ale.

Toward the end of term, he challenged the Textual Studies class members to submit suggested edits for his *Shakespeare and Text*; he was working on the revised edition. He even offered a prize to the winner. Letting my nerd flag fly, I took up the Early Modern gauntlet and submitted about thirty-six ideas of things he might clarify or add. I was so chuffed to learn that I'd won (though it turned out I was the only student who submitted anything). Still, I received the signed editions of a few of the Early Modern plays he'd edited with as much pride as if I'd just accepted an Olivier at Guildhall. I practically burst when he told me that he intended to incorporate several of my suggestions into the new edition. I experienced transcendent joy when I held the new version in my hands and read the acknowledgements in which he thanked me by name. I often wonder if anyone at KCL read those acknowledgements.

Martin, who very rarely gave any feedback to anyone in class, pulled me aside after one of my presentations in *Play & Poems*. My presentation partner had done very little on a very momentous play about a Dane, and as in many group projects during my MBA, I carried much of the weight and handled some sharp, challenging questions very adeptly.

"That was *very* well done, Diane." He might as well have handed me a Nobel Prize as I floated out of Marie Corelli's sitting lounge in which we held our sessions.

Gaspard-Gustave de Coriolis, a 19th-century French mathematician, thought about work a lot, too. Through extended study of the transfer of forces in rotating systems (think waterwheels), de Coriolis concluded that W=Fs, where W is work, F is force, and s is displacement. In other words, when we exert an effort on an object, we transfer energy to it. I exerted the following energy on the body of Shakespeare scholarship: five essays, five in-class presentations, twelve published theatrical reviews, two book contributions, three presentations at academic conferences, and one final dissertation.

I could not even estimate the number of hours that went into that oeuvre, but even the most miserable ones were joyful because I was, indeed, doing what I loved. If and when future students feel compelled to examine Shakespeare's non-expository opening scenes, my dissertation sits waiting in the Shakespeare Institute Library's archives, one slim sapling in a forest of imposing tomes.

Pacing around the living room in the disappointing place I rented on returning to Connecticut, I circled my laptop as if it were either a beast of prey which I needed to fear, or an oracle preparing to tell me my future—or both. I knew when the grades would be released, and just like a high school senior waiting for acceptances and rejections to drop, I intended to log onto the University of Birmingham student portal at that precise moment.

Like a rubbernecking motorist wanting to look but not wanting to look at a roadside crash, I logged on and, with hands shaking and stomach churning, scrolled to and highlighted the title of my dissertation. And then clicked.

When the message loaded, I blinked, as if they were fooling me. *High Merit*, it read: the equivalent of a B+.

My shoulders sank with my spirits. I could hear my father's voice as clearly as if he stood behind me, peeking at the screen. "That's great, honey, I'll wonder what it would have taken to get an A, but that's great!" Damning me with very faint praise.

I had poured every ounce of effort and knowledge that I

could have into my dissertation, and felt I had produced work deserving a Distinction, which would have equalled an A. It gutted me. I cried. I couldn't even tell anyone. The pressure my father exerted on me to succeed, according to his unrealistic standards, left me always feeling like I needed to prove something to someone, and a B+ wasn't enough. I felt I'd disappointed him. Disappointed myself. Disappointed some amorphous, nonexistent panel of Mount Olympus judges. The unrealistic expectations I'd set for myself were simply unattainable.

It felt like the marker had scrawled a big red "F" on the title page, even though the results came through electronically. At that moment, no part of de Coriolis's equation mattered to me. None of the philosophers' words resonated. I could focus *only* on the grade, which my history and old tapes that played in my head made inadequate. It was my *be all and end all.*

I licked my wounds for a week and finally messaged my three best friends at the Institute. Liz and Joe (*mature* students, like me) had gotten similar marks, and were similarly upset. Liz and I had developed a game plan by which we'd set progress goals and checked in with and supported each other throughout the gruelling process. This hit us hard because we had exerted such Herculean efforts to produce these opuses. Hannah, my brilliant pink-haired twenty-something friend, had fared better, rightly so. I knew her thesis, I knew the type of work of which she was capable. I felt deeply proud of and happy for her, but a part of me that I did not like also felt jealous and short-changed.

If KCL had accepted me and I'd attended, I would never have had the kind of rapport I enjoyed with the faculty at the Shakespeare Institute. The admiration and respect I felt for them prevented me from acting on the thought that consumed me: I wanted to reach out to express my frustration over the mark. I felt very lucky to have developed close relationships with many of them, including John, Martin, Erin Sullivan, and

Chris Laoutoris—the personal tutor who had introduced me to *Emblems* and supported my thesis scholarship. I knew I would not have become so close with the faculty in a typical university configuration. I had friends studying at KCL, and not only had they not studied every play, poem, and sonnet, but they barely saw their lecturers outside of the classroom in their more traditional university setting.

I also knew that, as in the case of the broken boiler, students are not as apt to challenge their professors in England as they might be in the States. I thought about this long and hard, wanting neither to exploit those relationships nor to sound like a big bunch of sour grapes, before I composed brief notes to Martin and John about my mark. Martin, who was, after all, my thesis advisor and had reviewed the work in process, noted that the reader who graded it was, unfortunately, neither of the two professors most familiar with my work, those who had supported it most fervently. An excellent academic in her own right, she researched and wrote about topics completely unrelated to mine, and she had no input or involvement in my research or writing.

"I had nothing to do with the distribution of dissertations to readers," Martin wrote. "Many factors influence the assignments. I would not have expected that she would read yours, and frankly, being intimately familiar with your work, I would agree that the grading might have been more generous. But the appeal process is rigorous, and the discrepancy is not glaring enough to proceed, in my opinion. You did good work, Diane."

John responded similarly. "I didn't read the thesis, and you know she has a reputation as a tough marker. But, Diane, I know your work. It is high quality. And honestly, should *that* grade from *this* institution disappoint you? Far from it, I think you should feel very, very proud."

I realised that I still seem to care what my father would think, even as an adult, even more than twenty years after he died. I thought I had freed myself of the constraints of his approval when I sailed, at age 19, from New York to Australia, New Zealand and back on a German container trip. A different journey with the same message: cut the cord; revel in your successes; stop listening to his voice in your head. It shocked me to still hear his voice; to know that I still cared—that it still mattered to me. I needed these surrogate fathers to remind me not to listen to the nagging voice of my biological one's ghost.

These venerated men who, in some ways, sat in my father's place, challenged me in a way they had all year. "What's in a grade?" they asked. Contrary to what Buddhism had taught me, I had erroneously attached all the value to the singularity of the outcome: to one grade.

Truly, I sat smiling atop Maslow's hierarchy triangle. Nothing I had ever accomplished in my life, save birthing two boys—which required an entirely different type of labour—gave me so much satisfaction. The base of the triangle that supported this euphoria was the *work*—the *effort*—that I'd expended over the magical year in Stratford Upon Avon. My initial disappointed reaction presupposed that it's the reward—the Oscar, the Nobel Prize—that validates the work. While such recognition brings with it meaningful material rewards in the form of income, job opportunities, and sponsorships, I neither needed nor craved those types of validation. The process and resulting self-actualisation were, in and of themselves, the prize.

I comb the crescent of Compo beach for sea glass regularly. Although I've never left empty-handed, sometimes I find only a few small pieces. Some might say that such a walk was a failure. I could not disagree more. The journey itself is the reward.

Shakesmen

Those vaunted academics at the Shakespeare Institute who so generously shared their knowledge with me and deeply influenced my thinking on Shakespeare and beyond.

Chapter 5:

Existentialism
(on identity)

"My excellent good friends!"

Hamlet (II.ii.197)

Jean-Paul Sartre famously thought hell was other people. In his play *No Exit*, the characters in the windowless, mirrorless room can only see themselves in the others' eyes. But what if heaven, too, were seeing yourself reflected back by those around you? If recognising yourself in others brought out your best self? It can, I suppose, do either or both, depending on the time of day, or the time of life.

In SUA I felt more like myself than I had in—well, since I could remember. It's hard to articulate exactly what that meant: it did *not* mean I was always happy or without stress. Attempting to describe it results in a flurry of inadequate clichés: I felt comfortable in my own skin; I felt at home; I felt seen and heard; I felt like I'd found my tribe.

This quest for identity via those around me smacks, on the surface, of selectivity, snobbery, or self-indulgence. Coveting a cohort that mirrors our own sensibilities is a razor's edge that can lead to racism, sexism, ageism, and a whole potentially dangerous set of -isms. But at the same time, it's natural and not necessarily nefarious to crave companions and activities that, to use Sartre's imagery, mirror our own interests and values. This pursuit, rather than narrowing our worldview, expands it by motivating, calming, and bringing out the best in us. It can lead to self-actualisation rather than self-indulgence.

This is what I found on the banks of the River Avon. I found, in the ultimate cliché, me. I recognised myself in the place and the people in a way that I had not in the Green Mountains of Vermont, the skyscrapers of New York City, the sunshine of Los Angeles, or the coastline of Connecticut. This pursuit of self and purpose does not necessarily require a change of venue. It does require both external and internal examination. My mother always said that "you take yourself with you wherever you go." Although I'd often joked that the odyssey to Shakespeareland was my version of a midlife crisis, it was not escapism so much as a journey of self-discovery.

It was not just one thing that allowed me to see myself there: not the hallowed ground, the graduate school, the classmates, the country, but a mosaic as complex as the patterns of stone that made up the streets of Stratford and the floors of Shakespeare's family homes. Myriad threads there wove the tapestry that made me feel so plugged in and turned on.

"Magic mirror on the wall, who is the fairest one of all?"

Misquoted as often as Hamlet gazing at Yorick's skull ("I knew him, Horatio," *not* "I knew him well"), the Evil Queen from the 1937 animated *Snow White* relies on her mirror for vital information. But when it does not reflect the answer she craves, she turns violent. Her mirror tells an unexpurgated truth. And, as Jack Nicholson's character Colonel Nathan R. Jessup knew in *A Few Good Men*, we cannot all handle the truth.

In Howard Beach, Queens, where I went to elementary school PS 232, Susan and I lived a floor from each other in one of the five-story red brick buildings of Lindenwood, where planes flew so low approaching or departing JFK that we could read their names on their tails. We would sit on the floor of either of our two-bedroom apartments—turned now, I understand, into high-end co-ops—and play out elaborate domestic scenarios with our Barbie dolls. We took turns being teacher and student with makeshift desks and imaginary chalkboards, grading each other's "work" with friendly objectivity. We concocted elaborate dishes in our "kitchens" on the asphalt playground adjacent to our building using forsythia blossoms and partridge berries. We rode our banana seat bikes around the pink concrete oval that formed an erstwhile courtyard for the quartet of buildings identical to ours. We were egoless friends whose mothers played mahjong and walked us to PS 232 together. We had no pretences, no social media to tell us how we should look in those halcyon years, and nothing to compete over. We saw the best in each other (notwithstanding the occasional tiff over who could be Catwoman for Halloween).

In high school, two close friends anchored me in the swaying seas of adolescence. A member of neither the elite cadre of cool kids nor the unfortunate bottom-feeding losers, I sat comfortably, as my older son once said, in the middle class of the social strata. Lauri, Sharon, and I would spend hours in one of their homes during the sultry summer hours sipping over-sweetened iced tea and talking about boys. When we were apart, we reconnected by phone the moment we walked in the door. We'd monopolise the sole house phone line, stretching the coiled mustard yellow or olive green cords to their limits, straining to take the receivers as far from the prying ears of our parents or siblings as we could. On weekend nights during the school year we'd sit in friends' darkened, panelled basements drinking bad beer that someone's older brother had passed to us through subterranean windows, listening to Pink Floyd, Yes, and Bad Company on cheap stereo systems. I attended enough parties in my leotard bodysuits and low-cut "peanut" pants and had enough friends to sit with at lunch that I felt accepted. I didn't want to drive in the faster lane of the A-listers among which rumours of sex and substances, for which I was unprepared, swirled.

The mirrors in college only got better and brighter. Though at first I treaded water in a strong undercurrent of not belonging—preppy LaCoste-wearing folk clearly came from a different suburb than I, one where whales swam happily on the wide wales of corduroy slacks—I scrambled to erase my New Jersey roots with a quick call home to my mother, who rushed to Daffy Dan's to procure and send several turtlenecks and faux Fair Isles so I could better fit in.

And I found my people. Or people who I thought were my people.

Randy was my anchor: assigned as freshman roommates, we met the moment we arrived, then lived together for four straight years. She hailed from a similar suburb and was also Jewish (at the time, Middlebury was not exactly a haven for the Hebrews). Together, we navigated the ultra-preppy waters, establishing a bulkhead of our own, constructed with a mix of New York area sensibilities and small New England liberal arts college. We fell in easily with two groups: our February Freshman and the entire football team and their fraternity, Delta Upsilon, because we all majored in Economics together.

As "fresh meat," they invited us to all their frat parties, the floors sticky with spilt keg beer.

These connections promoted me to upper-middle class, and the combination of social cache and intellectual stimulation only increased my bravado. After those parties, we would wander, buzzed, down to Duke's Deli at the edge of that small Vermont berg and, with nary a care for calories, carry Italian subs and Coke back to the TV room in our dorm building. The television tethered to the wall and spare, uncomfortable, indestructible seating betokened prison more than bucolic college, but we couldn't care less as we cosied up to each other to watch *Saturday Night Live* in its infancy.

I may have been feeling myself, but the athletic frat boys turned out to be more distorted funhouse than vanity mirrors. It *was* vanity and naiveté that made me admire my image, distorted in their eyes. The quest for popularity clouded my vision and deluded me into thinking those curvy mirrors reflected me accurately. Fortunately, a few truer reflections made it through that hype: I could see myself in John Bertolini's literature classes and Paul Cubeta's Shakespeare seminar—no need to preen in front of the mirror like I did for the boys. In those musty classrooms, my brain did all the reflecting, and I liked what I saw.

Sadly, graduation dropped a curtain on both the accurate and inaccurate self-images. I'd opted, largely to please my father, to pursue a business career. I neither wanted that nor had any real idea what it meant. It was as if he'd draped my mirrors in fabric emblazoned with the MetLife logo, all blue and white (coincidentally, Midd's colours, too), as he proudly paraded me around the building where he—and now I—worked.

Observant Jews cover all mirrors in the home with black cloth when they sit shiva for a departed loved one because it helps them stay focused on their mourning. This seemed apt as I now realise that I was mourning for myself as I travelled down a road of international employee benefits consulting and the pursuit of an MBA rather than joining Robert Frost on the road less travelled toward literature land. This occlusion of my self went hand in hand with the beginning of my lifelong partnership with anxiety. I knew I had pleased my father and was on some level happy to be part of an elite management training program at MetLife. The other chosen few looked and sounded a lot like the classmates I left behind at Middlebury; they hailed from clone institutions like Amherst and Smith. Although they might have been wearing 80s power suits with shoulder pads that went on forever, they may as well have worn layered Izod shirts, starched collars standing at attention, saluting the almighty dollar and the twenty-something 1980s New York City lifestyle.

The respite from this buttoned-up corporate life in which I excelled but did not recognise myself came on the weekends. We would mimic Madonna's style and dance until the wee hours of the morning at Danceteria or the Limelight with the beautiful underbelly of the city. I felt more like myself in glitter and lace, moving almost involuntarily to a throbbing new wave baseline: *Don't you want me baby?* The Human League made me feel human again, until Monday rolled around, and I went back to be ground by the grind.

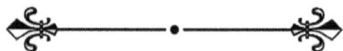

In 1984, a consulting firm invited me to join their Los Angeles office. Although the brown band of smog that planes plunge through on their approach to LAX might obscure it, the sun shines brightly in Southern California. Everything looks better when it's sunny and 72 degrees. The Vitamin D boost brightened my perspective, at least for a while.

Although the job consulting with large multinationals resembled what I did for MetLife after the training program, the change of venue—and absence of my father in the hallways—made it feel like a fresh new start. For a long time, I felt and acted like a tourist; the sensory stimulation of the new always recharged me—as it would do in SUA.

I also transferred from the MBA program at NYU—which I'd started before Johnson & Higgins (J&H) recruited me to the West Coast—to Pepperdine and took classes in the evenings. I dated two men long-term (not at once) during that time: Alain, a French transplant who looked like Alain Delon, and Michael, a manager at J&H who resembled Billy Dee Williams.

They were both very different from anyone I'd ever dated before in background, education, and experiences. Those superficial differences, like their celebrity good looks, blinded me momentarily (especially in film industry-obsessed Tinseltown) and made me feel like a Hollywood starlet.

Their appeal quickly faded once I saw beyond their shiny movie-set facades. In both cases, white grainy substances clouded the illusion: Alain's family had a tile installation business that he planned to take over; he'd enrolled in the MBA program to learn how to manage it more professionally. He felt that grout would cement our relationship—he thought I'd be a great addition to the family business. He lived at home with his parents and older brother, and I sensed that he'd be happy for me to join them. While I admired the hard work they'd put into creating a successful tiling enterprise, I didn't aspire to join their family business. I wanted a life of the mind.

Michael, with a future as bright as his gleaming smile, wanted to bond over another white powder: cocaine. Both were, for me, deal breakers, and when the white dusts settled, neither of them remained in the picture.

And then came Donald.

We waited in the salad bar line at the Four Seasons Dallas. Even as he stood behind me, I could sense his presence.

He'd been teaching the session I'd attended all morning on designing pay plans. Towers Perrin, another consulting firm, had persuaded me to leave J&H to come do international employee benefits and compensation consulting with them, and my compensation skills needed sharpening. A well-known compensation consultant at Towers and beyond, he figured prominently in the curriculum. And in my daydreams. He was not only clearly extremely bright, but also quite delicious looking.

The training session attire guidelines read "casual." To him, that meant slacks and a golf shirt. To me, it meant a short denim skirt and black T-shirt that had some splashy pink-and-white design on the front. I'd tied my hair back with a rolled-up white bandana, and I wore white Converse high tops and scrunched-up socks. The look was more Madonna wannabe than up-and-coming professional, but this was in the days before anyone had clearly defined "business casual." I screwed my courage to the sticking place, and despite the hideous outfit that tried to persuade me not to, I turned around, stuck out my right hand, and said:

"Diane Meyer. From the LA office in international comp and benefits. I really enjoyed your presentation this morning." So smooth. *And you are very easy on the eyes, too,* I didn't say out loud. At least I hoped I hadn't.

"Don Lowman," *I know,* "New York," *I know,* "nice to meet you. That's quite a strong handshake," he said. He would comment on how much that impressed him for decades to come. Fortunately, he never mentioned the scrunchy socks.

"I'd like to talk to you, actually." *Me? Really?* "I have an offer to manage the compensation unit at the LA office, and I've never been there. Maybe you could tell me more about the office and the area. But you can't tell anyone. This is in the early stages and is confidential."

My lips are sealed, I thought, and tried not to think too hard about his. *Be professional, Diane. This man may be devastatingly handsome, but he outranks you.* What I said was,

"I'd be happy to show you around," and made sure to give him my number (home, that is; cell phones were not ubiquitous in 1987).

I planned that day like a professional tour guide. I took him to the Hollywood Boulevard Walk of Fame, the LA County Museum of Art, and the La Brea Tar Pits. We paused for a mid-morning break on Melrose Avenue, where we both ordered iced teas in which we each put two packets of fake sweetener.

"I drink so much iced tea!" I said.

"Same. I never thought anyone drank as much as I did!"

I commented on the Angelinos' obsession with cars and identified the different models cruising by.

"I can't believe that you know the difference between a Saab 9-3 and a 9-5," he said.

I told him I'd been a DJ on our college radio station, and he revealed his fanaticism for The Who. I think I may have sealed the deal when I told him I knew the lyrics of "Quadrophenia" by heart. He was incredulous and tested me.

"5:15," he laid down the gauntlet.

"Girls of fifteen sexually knowing the ushers are sniffing eau de cologning the seat are seductive celibate sitting pretty girls digging prettier women."

Maybe he thought "Sea and Sand" was more obscure.

"Here by the sea and sand nothing ever goes as planned I just couldn't face going home it was just a drag on my own."

He just stared at me. He dug deep, thinking maybe I'd just gotten lucky. "Dirty Jobs."

"I'm being put down I'm getting pushed round I'm being beaten every day my life's fading things are changing I'm not going to sit and weep again."

He smiled. I passed the test. I *had* just gotten lucky.

I took him to Venice Beach to soak in the quintessential SoCal coastal experience. We ogled the oiled weightlifters at Muscle Beach and dodged scantily clad rollerbladers on the sandside path. We dined there in the nearby Rose Café, which stands to this day.

"I can't believe you. Intellectual, business-savvy, culturally engaged. And you like The Who. What am I missing?" he said.

What I'm missing, I thought, *is a man like you.* I felt like I was sitting across from a brightly lit vanity mirror, bulbs affixed to its perimeter, illuminating an image I'd hoped to see of myself for so long. Who's the fairest one of all? At that moment, he made me feel like it was me.

We sat in a chi-chi Greenwich restaurant, examining the cutlery and the menu; anything to avoid eye contact. My parents had agreed to stay with the boys. Everyone could sense the crackly tension in the air, and they hoped a night out would do us good. I hadn't dressed up in a long time. Put real makeup on in a long time. Left Westport in a long time. I allowed myself the illusion that the prettying-up and getting out of town might somehow brake what felt like a juggernaut hurtling toward divorce court. I lifted my eyes and my glass of chardonnay.

"Happy anniversary."

"This isn't a celebration. It's a dinner." He'd picked up neither his eyes nor his glass.

My shoulders fell and bile rose into my throat. I went through the motions of ordering and eating and making inane chit-chat—or, really, listening to him talk about himself, as he usually did when we had a "date night," staring somewhere over my head but not looking me in the eye. I wanted to throw up not only the food, but any illusion I'd ingested that our life together might be salvageable.

The mirror had cracked. Or, more accurately, I could no longer see myself in mirrors at all. I had become a vampire. Someone or something had drained, slowly, the lifeblood from me so that I lost my reflection completely. I had spent so many years trying in vain to please and seek approval from him that

I had virtually no idea what I even looked like anymore.

That night in Greenwich I felt only fear and incredulity. What would become of me and my boys? Was he involved with someone else? How would I survive this trip off the cliff into divorcéehood?

Slow digestion of this new dawning reality allowed me to move from abject terror to objective acceptance. I thought about how I had minimised almost every aspect of myself to maximise the image of *the good wife*. A slide show of subjugations played in a loop:

I am costumed in silly golf clothes and shoes standing by a set of shiny new clubs. Trying desperately to make arms that I knew were connected to both my body and brain mimic the swing that Donald had demonstrated. But feeling more like Olive Oyl than Nancy Lopez. Riding in the cart with him for eighteen holes at countless golf courses while he swore and scowled over bad shots.

I wait with a toddler at my side and an infant in my arms in the window in McLean, Virginia, waiting for his car to come up the road. "I'll be home by 5:30" inevitably turned into 7:00. I felt like all I did was wait, exhausted, for him to come home, to help, to play with the boys, but it happened rarely. He had an important call, an essential meeting, a crucial project, an important client, a last-minute trip. He was indispensable and available to everyone. To everyone but us.

Waiting became my default posture. Waiting for him to be present, but not wanting to upset him by asking.

I sat at the beach with two young boys on the summer weekends, having schlepped approximately a ton of sand toys, sunscreen, towels, and cooler-encased snacks down to the shoreline. I eyed with envy the tidy families of four that included fathers who made sandcastles with or tossed Nerf footballs to their toddlers. Donald couldn't be with us because he would play golf at a club that disallowed women and children because he'd worked hard all week and it was good for business relationships. What, I wondered, about our relationship?

Heaven knows I wasn't perfect. It takes two to tango to the end of a marriage. Resentment bred in me a short temper and proclivity for snarkiness. I don't know who was the chicken and who was the egg, but at that point it hardly mattered.

I touched the brushed nickel doorknob that opened the unlocked door from the garage to the mudroom. It may as well have shot Tesla coil orb bolts of electricity because I felt freedom and relief radiate through my fingers and up my arm. The jolt expanded my lungs with the fullest, deepest breath I'd taken in over a year.

I had no discernible reason to feel so grounded. The man I (still) loved, with whom I had built a life and created two beautiful children, had moved out that day. Months of resentment and animosity eroded those very foundations with the same force that the eleven years of Compo Beach tides smoothed rough rocks into skimming stones.

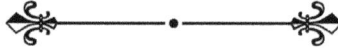

I had been laughing—and doing most everything else—to please others, including Donald, for so long that I no longer knew what I actually found funny, interesting, or satisfying. We all present different selves to different people at different times. It's a social exigency. But if you do it too often, or if the selves have too little to do with the "real you"—hard to define, easy to experience—you misplace yourself.

The relief came because I knew that when I opened that door, I could genuinely be my own sad, anxious, worried self. I had, for so long, tried to find the right ingredients in the right combination that would bake me into a satisfying dish for him—The Good Wife Stew—that it all but consumed me and left me alone without myself.

The transporters on the USS *Enterprise* could scramble the Star Trek crew's molecules and reconfigure them on the surface of planets far, far away. Music can just as rapidly and efficiently take us to another place and time. It can also smooth a balm on angst and trauma. Shakespeare called it "the food of love" (*Twelfth Night*, I.i.1). A generation later, William Congreve, another English playwright, claimed that "music hath charms to soothe the savage breast. To soften rocks, or bend the knotted oak."

The Lovin' Spoonful plants me squarely at the Howard Beach, Queens community pool in 1966 whenever I hear their "Summer in the City." The scents of Coppertone and grimy sweat filled the humid air. Moms protected their beauty parlour beehive hairdos with latex bathing caps festooned with faux flowers. From under those rubber blossoms, they protected their kids with gazes as sharp as their pearl-pink painted nails. Susan and I swam in the pool, aswarm with toddlers and tweens, or danced "the swim" on the concrete deck that singed the soles of our feet. Cousin Brucie blasted this and other top twenty hits in predictable rotation from our compact, battery-powered transistor radio. As long as no one splashed it with over-chlorinated water. He, like the artists that recorded them, knew they had the power to assuage tween angst, and it did ours.

Music had made me feel seen and heard and healed so often in my life and had provided soundtracks to significant life transitions and eras. Naturally, it did the same as my marriage dissolved in the late aughts: what I saw as my divorce playlist looped on repeat on the radio in our Lexus LX470—an SUV that made me feel Lilliputian. The songs stuck in my mind long after I gently let myself down from the lofty front seat. I felt these artists spoke to me directly as surely as a heartbroken middle school girl believes Taylor Swift is strumming their pain with her fingers.

Chester Bennington of Linkin Park knew that I felt numb; that I was so tired of being what Donald wanted me to be; that I didn't know what he expected of me; that I felt every step I took was another mistake to him. The Ramones knew I wanted to be sedated. Harvey Danger knew that I wasn't sick, but I wasn't well; that I was in Hell. And Amy Lee of Evanescence knew that I was so tired of being here, suppressed by my childish fears. Knew that if he had to leave, I just wished he would leave.

I cried tears of incredulity, of failure, of desolation when these and so many other artists sang my words from their mouths. I just hoped the boys didn't notice from their spots in the back seat. But also, I felt so seen.

These tunes said what I couldn't verbalise; seemed to see through the car tuner to the rear-view mirror, where I watched the vision of the future I'd envisioned fade in the distance, but could see myself more clearly. Warning: objects in the mirror may be closer than they appear. Maybe I was finally approaching myself.

I finally flew across the pond in August 2017 to begin my adventure. I tumbled out of the car from Heathrow in the early morning at the steps of the Avonlea B&B, jet-lagged and jittery with adrenaline. I knew it was well before check-in time, but owners Clare and Rob greeted me graciously. Rob schlepped my two overstuffed purple rolling Land's End duffels up the narrow staircase while Clare led me to my room. It was too late for breakfast but too early for official check-in, and I was too keyed up to sit down, anyway. I knew if I allowed myself to close my eyes, I'd fall deeply asleep and really wreck my circadian rhythm.

Instead, I set out to explore my new environs. In crossing

the Clopton Bridge over the Avon, I found myself at the foot of the Gower statue, commemorating not only the Bard, but four of his most famous characters: Prince Hamlet, a hand-wringing Lady Macbeth, the jovial Falstaff, and young Prince Hal. Shakespeare sat atop looking down not only on his creation, but upon the whole town from which he hailed, and which he had put on the map. Standing there, temporally disoriented, I reeled remembering standing in that exact same spot 26 years prior with my new husband on our honeymoon.

I felt as if the transatlantic trip had erased all that and subsequent history and afforded me the proverbial clean slate to start anew. Not only had I changed venues, but I had completely changed my cohort. And the beauty of this new band of brothers (and sisters) was that we were *all* new to each other. We would learn each other's curricula vitae bit by bit, but none of us had preconceived notions about the others.

For me, it was like looking in a two-way mirror in an interrogation room (minus the crime). A crowd of onlookers may have scrutinised me from behind a large glass panel, but I could, initially, only see me reflected back at me on a pure, blank canvas. I felt as liberated as the butterflies that had freed themselves from their cocoons just across the river at the Stratford Butterfly Farm. And like them, I would find myself in a bubble with others who, while we may all have sported different wings, were of the species *Shakespeare-Obsessives*. I would live in this Shakespeare-centric town, where the Institute, Birthplace Trust, and Royal Shakespeare Company (RSC) shared my focus and passion. His image greeted me at every turn. This, for me, was Mecca.

I felt like the nerdy elementary school girl dressed up like a bee in Blind Melon's *No Rain* video. Laughed off stage in a school talent show in a dim auditorium, she finds liberation and acceptance in a bright, open field where she frolics with a group of revellers all dressed like bees.

<u>Shakespark</u>

*The flame that the Bard lit in me and my
fellow fanboys and girls.*

Chapter 6:

Equanimity

"Prithee peace!"

Macbeth (I.vii.45)

"The coming and the going, the to-ing and the fro-ing, the ebbing and the flowing." A disoriented, dishevelled woman wound toward us, flailing and ranting. I froze, my hands gripping the handle, ready to throw my body over the stroller and shield my nine-day-old firstborn son from this crone.

My mother and Donald flanked me, and we moved as a unit to give this woman a wide berth. It was they who had convinced me to make this foray toward the palm-tree-lined Westwood Boulevard in the always sunny-and-72 Los Angeles. We all needed a change of scenery and some fresh air, but this mama bear would barely let friends and family near her newborn cub without full-body sanitisation. Knowing this, they instinctively fell into formation to protect him. The woman just wandered past us, oblivious, this wizened witch opining on time and space.

"The coming and the going, the to-ing and the fro-ing, the ebbing and the flowing." I heard her words twenty-eight years later, walking alone down Henley Street in Stratford Upon Avon, where the Birthplace sits. The boy and his brother grown, the husband an ex, and my parents gone. The wattle and daub facade of the Birthplace remained untouched by well-intentioned Victorians who had "improved" some of the other buildings in town by painting the beams black and the plaster white. Its dull exterior made me glow warm with nostalgia.

I had to-ed and fro-ed from this place physically and mentally for decades. Leaving after the MA programme (I graduated in December 2018, after I'd left) felt like an amputation. I could certainly live without Stratford, but I preferred not to.

Every cobblestone, tuft of riverbank grass, and storefront was a tile in the intricate mosaic that illustrated my relationship with this place and myself. Each reflected moments in time that had moulded me. Seeing them now, having earned my degree, having returned as a civilian—not a student—afforded me a rear-view mirror perspective on my prior tenure here as I simultaneously looked forward. The coming and going had provided as much of an education as the education itself.

The same two living statues have performed on Henley Street at least as far back as the beginning of my studies. One, a chain-mail-clad, metal-helmeted, sword-wielding knight, reminds me of something out of *Monty Python and the Holy Grail*. The other, a head-to-toe white ghost of Hamlet the elder, recalls the twin albino wraiths in the *Matrix Reloaded*.

In full regalia, they stand stone still, engaged in a staring contest with some invisible adversary in the middle distance. They endure, unflinching, just like the Queen's (or now, the King's) Guards through wind and rain, freezing cold and blistering heat. Although both of them tolerate a great deal of gaping curiosity and attempts to make them break character, the Guards never do. But for a fee, the living statues will.

A pound coin dropped in the tin cans at the feet of their decorated soapboxes will animate them instantaneously. They, like Iago at the end of *Othello*, utter no words, but instead entertain their patrons with expressive pantomimes.

I have walked down that storied street before the shops open and before the tour buses arrive. Those men sit, yards from each other, on their as-yet-unfestooned stands applying makeup between sips of takeaway coffee and drags on hand-rolled cigarettes.

They are the same people as they are when in character, but they are not. This, then, was how I felt on returning to this place. I was the same person, but I was not. I, like them, had suffered the slings and arrows of outrageous fortune. They endured stormy weather; I'd endured my own personal tempests. Connecticut ennui. The uncertainty of what I will be when I grow up. Divorce. Losing my mother. Concern, always concern, for my boys.

Yet they, like me, return and commit to persevere come precipitation or sunshine. I appreciated the glimpse beneath their facade and the motivation that these unlikely role models provided for me to move forward.

Reception Theory, a literary concept introduced by the academic Hans-Robert Jauss in the late 1960s, framed my dissertation. It posited that literature's (or any art's) impact depends heavily on the reader/observer—the audience. Each observer's history, experiences, and even states of mind determine how they perceive the work as much as, if not more than, the work itself.

Returning to Stratford Upon Avon as a non-academic very much confirmed this for me. I had, I realised, vilified Westport and myself in it, and glorified SUA and myself in it. Like the living statues, though, we were all one in the same person regardless of dress or address. Neither version was inherently "either good or bad," as Hamlet said, "but thinking makes it so" (*Hamlet*, II.ii.212).

I could be happy and engaged or bored and frustrated in either or both places. Before this most recent fro-ing, Stratford represented halcyon days shot through gauzy, soft-focus cheesecloth. Westport conjured harshly lit, tight-angle, unflattering images.

Equanimity
/ˌekwəˈnimədē/
noun

mental calmness, composure, and evenness of temper, especially in a difficult situation.

It's what the British do, isn't it? Keep calm and carry on. So cliché. Yet after years of coming from and going to this country, observation and osmosis had finally made an inroad into my thick, stubborn skull. Brits seemed to viscerally understand that we cannot always control our circumstances, but we can control how we respond to them.

Buddhism frames the concept more spiritually, positioning *equanimity* as the steady, conscious realisation of transience, the acceptance of impermanence. It is the ability to observe without getting entangled; the spaciousness of seeing things from a loftier viewpoint. In filmmaking terms, it's the long, high shot.

Nowhere does this perspective come into such clear focus as on an aeroplane. En route back to England, flying out of JFK, I watched "the city" recede, its once stunning skyline now marred with the adolescent cystic acne of a spate of needle skyscrapers. I watched the shoreline near my home become nothing more than a beige ribbon bifurcating two pieces of fabric: the blue of the sea and the green of the trees. I waved goodbye to another underwhelming Mets season as we flew by Citi Field and marvelled at the mass of headstones at Forest Hill Cemetery. At a certain point, it became an aerial view of Mr. Rogers' Neighbourhood. It looked fake. From this perspective it was just a clever LEGO creation.

Just before we reached cruising altitude, I always thought: *Nothing matters*. I imagined yellow taxis and amorphous Ubers jockeying for position in the demolition derby that is New York City traffic. I envisioned automatons rushing up the sidewalks with preternatural urgency, autopilots with laser focus on iPhones and not the city's teeming humanity, hawkers handing out **$89 SUITS!!!** flyers, garbage piled high on the curbs, pizza by the slice. None of it got in their way as they rushed to their IPOs, or to nothing. They ignored *Do Not Cross* signs, as does every good New Yorker. How inane it all seemed from where I knew this with certainty: *Nothing matters*.

The clouds we climbed above finally obscured the distant view of the concrete maze. That moment always feels like a triumphant victory of both physics and fantasy. We'd risen above. We floated. Only the progress past the white cotton candy clouds confirmed our movement. So close that I could touch them, sure it was spun sugar and not condensed vapour. I could not see what I worried about anymore. My most immediate concern became which meal and which movie. The pasta. And *Top Gun*, two? Too?

And then we flew into darkness. Nothing. *Nothing matters*. But it did because we were inside it. Inside nothing. I shut my window shade per the head flight attendant's directive as she dimmed the cabin lights. Nothing inside or out. Maybe everything matters, but not enough to worry about as much as I do.

That same flight attendant, now an air angel flitting through my groggy non-slumber state, tapped me on the shoulder. She magically managed, she told me, to manipulate spacetime so that the meal (having replaced the sun and the hourglass as the definitive indication of time) was breakfast and would I like the omelette with ham—NO—or the yoghurt and granola—YES—and tea with milk?—please.

I peeked under the shade to watch the sun rise on a new day, new dawn, new land. Once our tray tables were stowed and seat backs returned to their upright positions in preparation for landing, I watched as the verdant, irregular mosaic of my destination came into view. And thought again, *Nothing matters*. I loved that the English farmers and shepherds felt no need to make right-angled land divides. Ancient stone walls and meandering hedgerows separate field from field, pasture from pasture. Myriad shades of green create this quilt to blanket the island with periodic seasonal variations: the wheat of recently harvested hay, or the bright yellow shocks of blooming rapeseed.

These flights epitomised equanimity for me. Rising above it all while maintaining awareness that it's all there. Nothing I could or needed to do about any of it.

This equanimity often exited via the plane's oval porthole as soon as we touched down at Heathrow. Please remain seated until the captain has turned off the fasten seatbelt sign. Where are you running to, anyway? Passport control will take forever to get through and as we are critically short-staffed baggage will take longer than that. Buh-bye, thank you, buh-bye. The traffic crawled on the wrong side of the road even at this god-awful early hour. I had to pee. I should have gone in the terminal. I was hungry. Was I hungry? Should I have been hungry? What time was it *really*?

Why was it so difficult to hold on to one of those cotton puffs I watched so wistfully? I somehow managed during my MA year. The magic of the place and the quest cast a spell on me; the distance from home let me view all the things I'd normally fret about as ant farms from high in the sky.

The to-ing and the fro-ing. I began my relationship with Stratford Upon Avon as a tourist initially. I visited with my mother in 1983 during a trip to see my sister who was spending her junior semester abroad in London. I sent Suzanne a postcard featuring all the town highlights and mentioned that we'd visited "the Bard's grave." In 1991, I returned on my honeymoon. Mentally, it's always been a magnet. A place that has drawn me to it, like a lighthouse beacon in the fog. This lighthouse, though, is not at the edge of the sea; it's in the heart of the country.

The globe. The Globe. The orb. The planet. The theatre. The head. A ball. A ping pong ball, I bounce gently back and forth over an ocean. To study. To visit. To plant a flag.

A pinball. I ricocheted around town, propelled by invisible flippers. Caroming into familiar bumpers. Initially, embracing the expatriate student life. We cheered England on during the Six Nations rugby tournament, raising our pints at each try; we mustered our collective mind power at weekly pub quizzes; we sat on shabby carpet eating crisps trying to kill each other playing *Werewolf;* we salsa-ed like our grades depended on it at The Other Place; we read poetry at slams; we sat on the lawn at the Dell to watch amateur troupes try their hand at the Bard; we frequented the Picturehouse, munching on sweet and salty popcorn watching everything Bergman and Studio Ghibli churned out; we day tripped to London to sit in the stalls at the thatched O and compare their board treading to that of the RSC; we followed the Greenway's old railway path past galloping horses at the raceway and meandering sheep in the pastures; we ventured to the nearby Cotswolds hills to ancient storybook market towns dotted with yellow sugar cube oolitic Jurassic limestone cottages; we hiked up to the Welcombe Hills obelisk to find the well where Ophelia's prototype drowned; we herded geese at Mary Arden's farm; we had our hands massaged with cream we could not afford at Jo Malone while we sipped complimentary champagne; we feted *our* Joe Malone with a chocolate-frosted cake in the shape of a penis in the back room at the West End; we cried and cried and cried when we said goodbye.

I promised to come back.

I had to come back.

I knew I would come back.

I came back. As a visitor, a year after I left, just before COVID-19 changed the complexion of the world. When I arrived in Stratford Upon Avon, I felt exquisite agony: I was Neil Diamond. Stratford was fine, but it wasn't home, Westport was home, but it wasn't mine no more. *I am, I said.*

My friends and I felt desperate to honour and commemorate our magical year—to immortalise it. We went together to a sketchy closed barber shop on Wood Street. A sketchy guy let us in as if for an impending drug deal or to access an underground unadvertised speakeasy. We walked past the barber chairs, barbicide, strops, and straight razors to a backroom. The tattoo parlour, where the masseuse-type table took up most of the space.

Rosemary for remembrance. Such an obvious choice that it reeks of cliche. This was my first—and only, to date. Late in life, it seemed, for such rebellion. It violated the laws of my Jewish forebears. I would defile my body such that I would technically disqualify myself from burial in Jewish ground; but who cared anyway? I wanted to be burnt to a crisp and scattered along the insignificant-enough-to-be-called waves at Compo Beach and on the docile, swan-swarmed waters of the River Avon.

We giggled like the children we saw in their uniforms on their way to primary school: slightly nervous tittering. Like some satanic ritual, this would seal our bond; set us apart together; ink us for eternity. The number three held such significance for me: my lucky number, and so much more. We, the holy trinity, had Pythagoras's perfect number of rosemary sprigs inked into our skin for eternity. It represented harmony, wisdom, and understanding. Trios abounded in Shakespeare: the number of witches in *Macbeth*, women in *Coriolanus*, and chests in *Merchant of Venice*...

I went first. Brave or unable to tolerate the anticipation, I whined like a toddler awaiting vaccinations. And just like during those visits to the paediatrician's office with my toddlers, it was over in a flash. My friends held my hands as I had held my sons'.

"That's it? You're done? That didn't really hurt." Then I held their hands as the needle pierced their skins, in turn, repeatedly, to seal the deal. Blood sisters wrapped in cellophane, on our way to Boots to buy Palmer's cocoa butter to apply as a balm to soothe our wounds.

That visit was so brief that I left the country before the tattoo fully healed, and worried that it might get infected and wondered what my boys would think of their old mom who still saw herself as a young student.

On the next visit I apologised to Phil for dragging him down to Heathrow so early as he dragged my duffle to the entrance at the side of the building.

"Don't be silly," he said. "That's my job. Do you need me to help you inside with this?"

"No, it rolls! Thank you and see you in a few weeks." Phil had become a friend over these years of to-ing and fro-ing. He caught me up on local and national gossip on each of our rides back to SUA. I knew he would use these early morning hours now that he'd finished working for the day to take his dog for a long walk along the canal, where houseboats drift, impeded only by the sets of locks they must manually manipulate to pass.

This drop-off, though, was special. He had deposited me at *my place*. Not a rented flat, not a friend's home, not the nearby B&B (whose owners Sue and Simon originally introduced me to Phil), but *my place*. COVID-19 brought with it many unwanted lessons, but also some wisdom. And that Hallmark Card, pop psych, toss away line for me, and many I know, was this truism: life is too short to not do the things that really matter to you while you can still do them. Propelled by how much we lost during the pandemic and how little time, relatively speaking, I might have left, I decided to take the plunge. To make our relationship permanent. To stop pining and whining and plant a small American flag in England's terra firma.

I bought a shoebox-sized flat in a sweet red brick complex that I'd walked by a hundred times en route to and from the train station: shaped like a bird with its wings spread out in flight, crowned with a working clock on a spire visible from blocks away, and open only to residents over age sixty.

I felt like a titillated interloper turning the latch to *my* building with *my* key—still incredulous, still expecting alarm sirens to sound. The narrow halls were quiet at that early hour as I made my way past the lobby that resembled that of a nursing home just a little bit too much. Florally upholstered furniture flanked by mediocre wooden case goods that recalled the uniquely scented homes of everyone's grandmother. A utilitarian galley kitchen with outdated, kitschy cabinets (found in my flat, too—originals, apparently) and cups and saucers set out for afternoon tea. A mid-construction jigsaw puzzle on a rickety card table that reminded me of the one my mother set out for mahjong night in Howard Beach.

A cluttered bulletin board announced the schedule for upcoming red clay roof tile repairs, the date for the Macmillan Cancer Charity tea, and adverts for La-Z-Boy-like loungers that propel the occupant up and out with the push of a button when their own muscles refuse to do the work. To the empty lift. Happy not to have run into anyone just yet; I needed to acclimate. The new kid on the block, decades younger than most residents, and a foreigner. An upstart crow of whatever the British equivalent of a snowbird would be. In a place where decidedly not much happens each day, my arrival and unusual residency would provide transient entertainment.

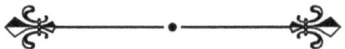

The flat, save for minor layout differences, could be the one I lived in diagonally across town as a student, down to the minute, windowless, and hence somewhat scary bathroom. I prayed that the air filter fan demons from College Mews hadn't followed me to haunt me here; I would have put contacting an electrician to perform a pre-emptive exorcism on my *To Do* list. The brand new ecru wall-to-wall carpeting and fresh coat of painfully neutral paint competed with the ornate wall sconces in the living and bedrooms and the baby-puke-mustard vinyl flooring in the 4x4' kitchen. Modern and updated, or sagging and in need of a facelift? The flat couldn't decide.

The large casement windows in both rooms opened outward, onto my realm: the little car park and Albany Road and greater Stratford beyond. My downstairs neighbour Janet set up an elaborate bird feeding and statuary station, much to my delight, just below my window. I sat on the windowsill and watched familiar and unfamiliar avian species nibble and wet/shake wet/shake themselves in the always-full birdbath. I even saw an elusive hedgehog nosing about one evening. I thanked Janet for the show by leaving bags of mealworms for her birdfeeders whenever I visited.

The residents' little cars sat tucked snug in their little spaces. Road size and fuel costs kept vehicle size to a surprising minimum here compared to the mobile living rooms that prowl the roads of suburban Connecticut.

Showered, unpacked, and ready to retrace my Stratford Upon Steps—albeit cognisant that I could not recreate the past—I descended to head out. A triumvirate of residents-cum-gate keepers greeted me—these three seemed at all times to flank the main entrance either on the stiff loveseat and matching chairs or at the sensible, utilitarian wooden table. They occupied the former and latter in the morning and evening hours, and the latter for tea at three, when they shared biscuits from a tin and gossiped.

"Are you the American?" said a dapper gentleman in a jumper that looked custom tinted to match his sky-blue eyes. He assumed the role of group spokesman; the couple behind him demurred, the husband eyeing me with kind curiosity, the wife with barely veiled suspicion.

"I'm Stan," he said, reaching out a hand for me to shake. Even at his age, which I estimated at 75, his strong grip impressed me. I later learned that he was 94.

I offered up my American hand. "Yes, I'm Diane. Flat 22."

"Are you sure you're old enough to live here, young lady? You know you must be 60." So, the welcoming committee *and* the security detail. I loved him immediately.

"I'm sure, Stan. Nice to meet you. Flattery will get you everywhere."

We became fast friends. I related the Campbell's condensed soup version of the story of why I was here that everyone seemed eager to know. I'd repeat it so often that I wished I could just push *play* on an anachronistic cassette tape player that surely some of them still had in their flats. The obsession with Shakespeare, the MA, the friends, the inexplicable need to be here, blah, blah, blah, not full time, just a few times a year. This resonated with those outside the building in greater

CV37 and 06880, but not so much with those inquiring Scholars Court denizens' minds.

This place was all but an assisted living residence; why would I choose it as my holiday home? To them, I was a curious, amusing enigma. When I finally passed muster, I passed through the front doors and crossed Grove onto Greenhill Street, my lungs filling with familiar molecules that lifted and energised me like Mentos seem to in their recklessly upbeat commercials—"The Freshmaker!"

The town, the streets, the sidewalks were all as familiar as the cliché back of my own hand, but at the minute, also very different. Subdued. The Queen, Elizabeth II, had died shortly before I arrived and would be memorialised shortly after. Only days ago, the SUA Facebook community posted photos of the RAF plane carrying her coffin traversing the skies above, transporting her from her beloved Balmoral to Westminster where her subjects would queue for days like crazed Beatles fans without the hormone-filled frenzy to catch a glimpse of and pay their respects to the only sovereign most of them knew in their lifetime.

I'd considered trekking to London for a fleeting moment, but my distaste for crowds and dirty port-a-loos dissuaded me. Besides, it felt right for me to mourn with my fellow Stratfordians. Every single storefront had removed or toned down their commercial displays (the charity shop windows sported clothing in shades of grey and black). Every one featured portraits of and kind words of gratitude for Her Majesty. I ran my hands over the raised *ER* embossed on a red, cylindrical post box, knowing that the next time I visited it might have changed to *CR*.

Her life flashed before my eyes as the portraits spanned the years from her 1952 acccssion to her recent 2022 Platinum Jubilee, marking a seventy-year reign—the longest of any monarch in the world. For once, SUA's focus had shifted from Shakespeare and the Elizabeth that sat on the throne and for whom he wrote to this second Elizabeth—the last British female monarch for the foreseeable future.

Both the Royal Shakespeare Theatre and Holy Trinity Church would live-stream the funeral proceedings; I felt lucky to have procured two tickets to the former. It felt so fitting and humbling to know I'd join this adopted community in bidding farewell to a figure who meant so much to them.

"I'm planning to wear something black, right?" I asked my good friend Liz, who would join me.

"Indeed," she said. "Something dark."

Attendees ushered us in, hushed, as if into a church. This cathedral to William Shakespeare had been converted for that momentous moment in history to Westminster. The screen upstage occupied the full height and width of the imposing stage. All darkly clad, all heads bowed, all eyes averted, all hands folded in laps with tissues at the ready. The proverbial pin-drop silence pierced only by an infant's cry—ushered out by his father who'd hoped but been unable to mourn with this crowd in communal silence. What sovereign would that baby know? Would the monarchy even still exist? Would his England, his Stratford, be the same as mine was as a new wife, an old student, and expatriate? Tempus Fugit.

Back at Scholars Court, the mood reflected the overcast skies. The sun might have been trying to poke through, but the clouds would hang over the West Midlands and beyond for some time.

Suzanne, the competent and cheerful house manager, had arranged the lounge seating theatre-style, like she did for movie night on Saturdays. The BBC still broadcast—long after the remaining rituals had gone private—the public aftermath of the funeral.

Wheelchairs and walkers that had yielded up their charges to the comfort of ugly upholstery waited like the Sovereign's Guard to accompany them back to their own resting spots in their flats. Stan, ever vigilant, greeted me like a Yeoman of the Guard as I crossed the threshold, his eyes damp behind steel-rimmed spectacles. He, I realised, would have remembered her father as King, would remember his equally elaborate coronation, his equally decorous funeral.

"Well, that's done isn't it?" he said. "Won't see another like her, will we?" He ended his statements with questions to which I nodded and shook my head respectively.

"Yes. No." The residents who had assembled to observe in hushed reverence and incredulity at where the time went reclaimed their external metal (and mettle) to make their way down the hallways, carpeting muffling their footfalls. Everything, including the pubs, had shut out of respect and to allow employees to join in the mourning gestalt. Stan couldn't even amble up to the now-shuttered Morrison's to do his daily grocery shopping.

I surveyed my new cohort—their metal appliances and joints and pins and dental bridges so different to the metal sported by my uni classmates: cartilage, nostril, nipple, lip, tongue, and navel piercings proclaimed individuality, rebellion, and sensuality. Steel, in both cases, steeling them against the slings and arrows of outrageous fortune; forming a fortress to protect them. For the youngsters, for something they wanted, hoped, longed, and looked for: individuality and agency. For the oldsters, against what they felt slipping away—being stolen—mobility, security, and independence. Freedom, I suppose, for both.

During these more recent visits, I'd spent less time sipping Guinness late into the evening and more sipping tea late into the morning. Making more pilgrimages to Argos and Asda for placemats and picture hangers than to the Warburg Institute to pore over ancient texts on emblems, but that was as it should be. The latter made me feel temporary; the former more permanent. Everything I loved about the place remained, even if some friends had relocated around the isle. I had changed and grown, but it still fit.

Having established this new way of being in both places, I have become a migratory bird. I have developed a pattern—the coming and the going. This repetition soothes me and provides perspective on both ends. The lines between absolutes blur and create equanimity that serves me in both places. Neither is good, neither is bad. The things that irritate me in one venue make me appreciate their foil in the other. The knowing that the one place is still there when I'm in the other creates a balance between the two that settles in my oft-fraught brain, in my oft-roiling belly. The balance between the two creates a surprising stasis.

I have aged and matured. I have grown younger. I did what my mother asked that I do eight years prior, as she died quietly. I started my life. There, *and* there, you are, I thought.

<u>Shakespeak</u>

The jargon that becomes vernacular for those steeped up to their ruff-collared necks in Shakespeare Studies.

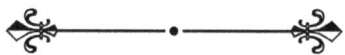

"See better"

King Lear (I.i.140)

Acknowledgments

I acknowledge the lovely shepherds at Atmosphere Press who held my hand and made my book better. Above all, I thank my son, editor, and coach, Dustin Lowman, who with preternatural talent, immense patience, and eagle-eyed acuity pushed me out of my comfort zone to encourage me not to settle for mediocrity.

About Atmosphere Press

Atmosphere Press is an independent, full-service publisher for excellent books in all genres and for all audiences. Learn more about what we do at atmospherepress.com.

We encourage you to check out some of Atmosphere's latest releases, which are available at Amazon.com and via order from your local bookstore:

Finding Us, by Kristin Rehkamp

The Ideological and Political System of Banselism, by Royard Halmonet Vantion (Ancheng Wang)

Unconditional: Loving and Losing an Addict, by Lizzy and Adam

Telling Tales and Sharing Secrets, by Jackie Collins, Diana Kinared, and Sally Showalter

Nursing Homes: A Missionary's Journey Through Heaven's Waiting Room, by Tim Eatman Ph.D.

Timeline of Stars, by Joe Adcock

A Boy Who Loved Me, by Wilson Semitti

The Injustice in Justice, by Charmaine Loverin

Living in the Gray, by Katie Weber

Living with Veracity, Dying with Dignity, by Alison Clay-Duboff

Noah's Rejects, by Rob Kagan

A lot of Questions (with no answers)?, by Jordan Neben

Cowboy from Prague: An Immigrant's Pursuit of the American Dream, by Charles Ota Heller

Sleeping Under the Bridge, by Melissa Baker

The Only Prayer I Ever Have to Say Is Thank You, by M. Kaya Hill

Amygdala Blue, by Paul Lomax

About the Author

DIANE LOWMAN is an award-winning essayist, memoirist, and poet. She served as Westport, Connecticut's inaugural Poet Laureate from 2019-2022. Her essays have appeared in many publications, including *O, The Oprah Magazine; Brain, Child*; and *Brevity Blog*, and she writes a regular column, "Everything's an Essay." Her first memoir, *Nothing But Blue*, was published in 2018.

Diane received her MA in Shakespeare Studies from the University of Birmingham's Shakespeare Institute in 2017. She has explored other forms of literary expression in more than 2,500 haiku and in essays on and reviews of Shakespeare's plays in various academic publications.

Diane teaches writing, Shakespeare, and yoga, and divides her time between her hometown of Westport, CT, and her home away from home in Stratford Upon Avon, England.

Milton Keynes UK
Ingram Content Group UK Ltd.
UKHW040639070923
428220UK00004B/184

9 781639 889143